GHOST HUNTING

IN MICHIGAN

BRADLEY P. MIKULKA

4880 Lower Valley Road • Atglen, PA 19310

Other Schiffer Books on Related Subjects:

Ghosts of Southeast Michigan
978-0-7643-3408-5

Michigan's Haunted Legends and Lore
978-0-7643-4240-0

Michigan's Haunted Nightlife
978-0-7643-3320-0

Designed by Molly Shields
Cover designed by Matt Goodman
Type set in Adobe Garamond Pro/Times New Roman

ISBN: 978-0-7643-4941-6
Printed in The United States of America

Published by Schiffer Publishing, Ltd.
4880 Lower Valley Road
Atglen, PA 19310
Phone: (610) 593-1777; Fax: (610) 593-2002
E-mail: Info@schifferbooks.com

For our complete selection of fine books on this and related subjects, please visit our website at www.schifferbooks.com. You may also write for a free catalog.

This book may be purchased from the publisher. Please try your bookstore first.

We are always looking for people to write books on new and related subjects. If you have an idea for a book, please contact us at proposals@schifferbooks.com.

Schiffer Publishing's titles are available at special discounts for bulk purchases for sales promotions or premiums. Special editions, including personalized covers, corporate imprints, and excerpts can be created in large quantities for special needs. For more information, contact the publisher.

Foggy Cemetery Background © zagzig. Tombstone And Graves In An Ancient Church Graveyard © tolgatezcan. Ballinskelligs Priory, Kerry, Ireland © Linda Caldwell. Spooky cemetery in the forest © llaszlo. Courtesy www.bigstockphoto.com.

DEDICATION

FOR THE SPIRITS.
MAY THEIR STORIES FINALLY BE TOLD.

CONTENTS

Preface...6

Guidelines: Investigating Cemeteries..7

Investigations..8

    Cemetery Near Maple Rapids...9
    A Cemetery Named Blood..14
    Ely Highway Cemetery..20
    Lovejoy Cemetery..29
    Purple Rose Theater..40
    Durand Union Station 49
    A Private Residence 61
    The Ohio State Reformatory (OSR)—Mansfield, Ohio 77
    Author Note: *A Haunting on Hamilton Street*......................................96
    Comedy Club 97
    The Stable 105
    Perry's Schuch Hotel..115
    Hoyt Library...121

Acknowledgments 128

PREFACE

For the past eighteen years, I have been a ghost hunter. For the sake of making things less confusing, in this book "ghost hunting" and "paranormal investigating" or "paranormal field" are interchangeable terms and mean the same thing. When my wife Brenda and I took over the SouthEast Michigan Ghost Hunters Society (SEMGHS)—one of the oldest ghost hunting groups in the state and based in Lansing, Michigan—there were exactly zero TV shows dealing with this subject. Today, it seems like every channel on TV has a program dealing with the paranormal. When we first started, people would look at us funny when we told them that we were ghost hunters and that we would romp through grave yards in the dark—doing this willingly and without hesitation. Nowadays, if people find out that you are a ghost hunter, some will immediately whip out their phones and show you their pictures from cemeteries or other haunted places they have been to. Don't get me wrong, we enjoy looking at pictures that people have taken. I just wanted to tell you how mainstream and popular ghost hunting has become.

There is one word that I absolutely hate in this field, though, and that word is "expert." An example of this would be: John is a ghost hunting expert. There is no such thing as an expert in the paranormal field! If you are an expert in a certain field, that means that you know everything there is to know about that subject. In ghost hunting, that just isn't possible. There are accepted facts that most people can agree on, but you learn as you go. We have been doing this since 1996, and we still learn from every investigation we conduct. We, as ghost hunters, simply do not have a book that can tell us everything that we need to know and how things are after someone dies.

Oftentimes, you will discover books about haunted places, but find that the author may have never visited the location he or she writes about. Sometimes, they will take information off the Internet and compile the story, adding in some of their own words. This book is not one of those types of books. Our group, or just Brenda and I plus our two children, have been to many places in our home state of Michigan and around this great country that have a reputation of being haunted or to have a certain level of paranormal activity. What follows are our true accounts of these places and the investigations that we have conducted there.

If you are the type of person who scares easily, before you continue reading any further, you might want to turn the lights on!

ENJOY.

GUIDELINES:
INVESTIGATING CEMETERIES

Cemeteries are a different beast to investigate, compared with other locations. When we investigate a house or business, the owners invite us in; but, in most cases (and there have been a few exceptions for us), the people who own a cemetery have not invited us. We are there on our own. There are a few guidelines one must follow when investigating a cemetery.

FIRST GUIDELINE: REMEMBER THAT PEOPLE ARE BURIED THERE.

These are not just tombstones sticking out from the ground. Each tombstone represents someone's mother, father, son, daughter, etc. You get the picture. Treat the cemetery with the dignity and respect that it deserves.

SECOND GUIDELINE: DO NOT VANDALIZE.

DO NOT—and I cannot stress this enough—destroy, vandalize, spray paint, or tear up the grass within cemeteries. You would be surprised how often this happens.

There is another local cemetery that we like to investigate and, one afternoon, we were driving by and there were some workers tending to the grounds. We stopped and started talking to them. They told us that the previous night some people were in the cemetery and they'd knocked over tombstones, left tire tracks in the grass, empty beer bottles on the grounds, and spray-painted graffiti on the church at the front of the property. Not only is this vandalism (you could be arrested if caught), but this kind of behavior hurts a ghost hunting group's chances of getting permission to be there after dark. I know of some cemeteries that will not allow *anyone* in after dark because of this kind of thing.

THIRD GUIDELINE: RESPECT POSTED HOURS.

Most cemeteries have hours posted showing the times that you can legally be on the property—usually dawn to dusk. Unless you have permission to be there after dusk, you are trespassing and the local police can and will issue you a ticket. If you do happen to get permission to be there after hours, make sure that you get that in writing and have it with you in case the police *do* make contact.

Since, anyone *can* go to a cemetery after hours, I will not be posting the address or exact location for the cemeteries that I will be writing about. (Nor will I will be giving exact locations for any homes or businesses that we have investigated, other than locations that allow the general public to either investigate or visit. This is for the safety of the location as well as for the reader.)

INVESTIGATIONS

CEMETERY NEAR MAPLE RAPIDS

When we first started our group in 1996, we began with investigating local cemeteries. The houses and businesses wouldn't come for a while. Don't get me wrong. I love a good cemetery and, sometimes, I prefer investigating cemeteries to other places.

Also, in the beginning, we didn't have the best equipment. Take our digital camera for example. It was short on pixels—not like the digital camera that we use today. So to say that our first digital didn't take very clear pictures may be an understatement. But you make do with what you have. It didn't even have a LCD screen on the back to look at the just-taken photograph. You had to hook it up to a PC with a cable and transfer the picture in order to view it.

Anyway, there was a cemetery near the town of Maple Rapids that I'd always wanted to investigate—I had heard stories... One day we took a little drive and ended up there.

The cemetery itself is situated in an area that has a few rolling hills. The far north of the property has a couple of moderate-sized mausoleums. I don't know the exact size of the entire cemetery, but I think five acres would be a safe estimate.

This particular visit wasn't an investigation per se and it was conducted during the daytime.

INVESTIGATIVE NOTE

Nighttime in a cemetery is something everyone who is into ghost hunting should experience. But you have to be careful if you are in a cemetery at night. Some of the tombstones are just high enough off the ground that you can trip over them and crack your skull open when you fall onto another tombstone. I advise people to go to the cemetery during the day, if possible, and see where the little ankle biters are. That's what I call those tombstones that you trip over. I also like to advise people to look down when walking and use a flashlight when at a cemetery at night.

A PERSON?

Brenda and I each went off in different directions. I was taking pictures as I went—not of anything in particular; just anything that I thought looked interesting. I found myself on a hill overlooking part of the cemetery and thought that this would be a good place to take a photo. Before I could take one, however, I noticed what looked like a person by one of the mausoleums. I could see Brenda was to my right, away from the mausoleum, and the kids were not with us. This cemetery is in the boonies and there isn't a house for a few miles, so it was unlikely that neighbors were around.

I decided that taking a picture could wait and I made my way to where I thought I saw the person. When I was in the general area, there wasn't anyone there I could see. I suppose it could have been shadows, trees, or bushes that I saw. I know I saw *something*; I just don't know for sure what.

Again, I walked around the cemetery just taking pictures and looking for the person who I thought I had seen earlier. I didn't see the person again and I wound up back at the spot on the hill that would provide a good photo op. I took a couple of pictures of the area and went to catch up with Brenda. We compared notes and came to the conclusion that the cemetery was quiet and we might need to make a return visit.

INVESTIGATIVE NOTE

One thing to remember: just because you don't get or see anything when you are at a location *doesn't* mean that there isn't anything there. What it *does* mean is that it was quiet when you were there and, for whatever reason, the spirits were not willing or able to make themselves known to you at that time. There are many factors that will give the spirits energy to do things or to be seen. All the factors have to be copacetic for an event to occur. Among the outside factors that will increase activity are as follows: a new or full moon, solar flares, geomagnetic storms, and a good old-fashioned thunderstorm with lightning can all give spirits their much needed boost of energy.

I will also add that we strongly believe that if a spirit doesn't think you can handle it (reasons unknown), it will not show itself to you. We feel that if a spirit can see and understand what is going on around it, and that if it doesn't like a person, or that person is making fun of the situation, then the spirit also will not make itself known to the person or group there. Doesn't that make sense?

As we walked back to the car, we thanked the spirits for allowing us to visit their graves. And since the spirits can and will follow you home, we asked them to stay in the confines of the cemetery.

Light coming from top of tombstone and heading into the sky.

It took me a few days after we came back from the cemetery to hook up the camera to the PC and transfer the pictures over. None of the pictures had anything odd or strange on them…except one. The picture that had something on it was one of the pictures I took when I was standing on the little hill and had a good view of the cemetery. The photo is of a tombstone. But the odd thing is that it shows a beam of light coming out of the tombstone and going up towards the sky.

The day was overcast with no rain, so it was not a weather anomaly. I can't explain the photo. I have tried to debunk it as being a ray of light from the sun, fog, and I even looked at the tree to see if it could have been a branch. None of those things are what is shown in the picture.

There was something else that happened to us after we came back from the cemetery. We think that one of the spirits didn't want to stay there and followed us home, even after we asked the spirits *not* to follow us. A few days after we came back, strange things started happening.

It began when our kids were in their rooms at night and our son told us that he could hear voices. We thought that he was just mistaking his radio for these voices. But he swore that he was hearing voices and not those from the radio. Then the dogs started acting strangely, too. They would look down the hallway and bark at something that we couldn't see. (Animals and children can see things that we can't. We have a saying that, "Your child's imaginary friend might not be imaginary.") These things at our home involved the little things that one can't always brush off as an overactive imagination or the dogs acting stranger than normal—and the next three things that happened can't be easily dismissed, either.

THE FIRST STRANGE HAPPENING

We had a friend over a week after the cemetery visit. When he was walking up to the front door, he saw a boy looking out the living-room window at him. When he came into the house, he asked where the boy was. We told him that our son was in his room. He said, "Not Sam; the other boy." We told him that there was no other boy in the house.

Our friend repeated that there had been a little boy looking at him when he'd walked up to the house. The boy had blonde hair and was wearing what looked like knickers with a white shirt. He just assumed that the boy was here to play with our son. He said that when he made eye contact with the boy, the child smiled at him.

We asked our friend if the boy he saw in the window was possibly a reflection from outside, or maybe a shadow from the trees. Our friend said, "Maybe—if a shadow can smile at you. Because our friend is a medium and can talk to the spirits, we asked him if the little boy was actually there or was he seeing him within his mind's eye.

Again, we were told that the little boy was there in the house and he was looking out the window at him. He went on to tell us that when he sees spirits, it is usually in his mind's eye, but he said, in this case, he actually saw the spirit standing in our house. He added that, as he was walking up to the house, he heard the little boy's voice whisper in his ear that his name was Petey. So, from that day our house guest was called Petey.

We asked our friend where Petey came from. He said that the child followed us home (though he didn't know from where) because he liked us. "He likes it at your house because you have kids." Petey didn't show up until after our trip to the cemetery near Maple Rapids, so we kind of put two and two together and assumed Petey followed us from that location.

THE SECOND STRANGE HAPPENING

Brenda's parents live kinney corner from us and two houses down. They can look out of their living room window and see the front of our house. A few days after our friend's visit, Brenda and our daughter Jessica were going over to her mom's house to pick her up to go somewhere. I followed them out to the car and, after they drove off, I went back into the house.

Jessica and Brenda arrived back home about an hour later. Brenda said that when they picked up her mom, she was surprised that Jessica was in the car. Brenda asked her mom why and this is the story her mom told her.

I was looking out my window at your house because I knew you were coming over to get me and I wanted to be ready to leave when you got here. I saw you and Brad come out of the house. There was a child that I thought was Jessica and she followed you out of the house. Brad held the door open and I saw the child go under his arm and go back into the house. I thought that Jessica had changed her mind and was going to stay home. Then I saw Brad go back into the house and then you pulled up in the car.

Neither Brenda nor I saw the child come out of the house and we certainly didn't see anyone go back into the house. Why her mom saw the child from their house and we didn't see it a few feet from us is unclear.

THE THIRD STRANGE HAPPENING

The last thing that we can't explain happened in the dining room. We have a sliding-glass door that leads from the dining room to the backyard, with vertical blinds covering the slider. Sitting in my chair in the living room, while watching TV, I have a clear view of the dining room and the slider.

I saw movement out of the corner of my eye coming from the dining room. Looking over to the door, I saw the blinds slowly swaying from side to side. There was no draft—since the slider was closed and we don't have AC. So there are no air vents that would cause the blinds to move. All of the pets were accounted for and they hadn't been near the dining room.

This happened on a handful of occasions. When I saw the blinds moving, I would say out loud, "Okay Petey, knock it off please." The blinds would slowly stop moving. Sometimes, after a few minutes, they would start again. I would again ask Petey to stop moving the blinds and they would slowly come to a stop.

It has been a long time since Petey made his presence known to us. We wonder what happened to him. Your guess is as good as ours. Maybe he just got bored with us and moved on to another place. It could be possible that he went back "home" to the cemetery. Petey is always welcome back at our house, though. We are still hoping that he comes back to pay us a visit. If he doesn't want to stay, we hope he can come back just to say "hi."

A CEMETERY NAMED BLOOD

This is a good example of how urban legends are born.

I have heard for years that Blood Cemetery was extremely haunted. There is one story that has been circulating around these parts since the early '80s concerning what happened to some teens one night at the cemetery.

It seems that four teenagers were in the cemetery drinking and something "chased" them out. Whatever it was chased them for miles and the teens blew through a stop light on a local road and were hit by an eighteen-wheeler. Three of the teens died instantly, but one survived and was rushed to a local hospital. A few days later, the lone survivor was interviewed and gave his account. What follows is supposedly the story the teen gave, but the story is from word-of-mouth and passed down through many people. The story I was told came from a friend who has lived in the area his whole life. This, I was told, came from the lone survivor.

Three of his buddies and the survivor were bored and wanted something to do. They, too, had heard stories about Blood Cemetery being haunted and figured this was a good enough time, if any, to go and check the place out. They found someone to buy beer for them and they drove to the cemetery, parked, and downed some beers. By this time they were getting brave, so they started to antagonize the spirits—if there *were* any—that were there. They said things like, "We are not afraid of you! If you have the b***s, come and hurt us! You're not tough; you're just a p***y," and things along that line. Nothing happened after they challenged whatever was supposed to be there and they were ready to call it a night and head for home.

They were talking about the cemetery and how it was a dud, that it wasn't haunted, and that there was nothing there. They joked that the story about the place being haunted probably got started because someone brought a girlfriend there and scared her, so she started the story to save face.

One of the boys said, "Let's blow this place," when they heard a noise coming from the caretaker's shack, near the back of the cemetery. They all looked in that direction and saw two red eyes looking straight at them. (They didn't have flashlights, so the eyes were not red because of a flashlight beam reflecting off them.) Then they heard a loud, deep growl coming from whatever it was that was near the caretaker's shack.

They were standing near their car and all of them took a step back when they heard the growl. One of them said, "Let's get the f**k out of here!" and they all hurriedly got into their car. The person driving started the car up and put the car in drive. The car wouldn't move. No matter how much gas he gave it, the car wouldn't budge.

One of them got out of the car to see if they were stuck on something. When he reached the back of the car, there was nothing that he could see that would prevent them from leaving. Then there was a rush of wind and he looked up and saw a creature, about seven feet tall with wings and glowing, red eyes—and it landed just a few feet from him.

He jumped back into the car and told the driver to "punch it!" This time the car spun its wheels and they started to drive towards the cemetery exit, finally leaving it behind, and heading towards town. The boy who had gotten out of the car told them about the winged creature and they looked back behind them. They all could see two red eyes... Whatever it was, they weren't losing it. The creature was right behind the car.

They drove for ten miles and, no matter how fast they went, the two red eyes were right behind the car. By this time, everyone in the car was freaking out. Something was chasing them and they didn't know what it was or even what it wanted from them. The driver continued to speed up, trying to loose the creature, but he couldn't. When they came up to the main road, the stoplight turned red, but the driver was so freaked out that he ran the light. That's when the eighteen-wheeler t-boned the car. The only survivor was seated in the backseat on the passenger side.

Supposedly, a few days after he told the police what had happened, he too passed away.

I have tried to research this story, but cannot find any local media—TV or newspapers—that have covered it. The person who told me the story swears that it really happened.

So my interest was piqued and, in the early 2000s, I did a Google search on the cemetery. There were 4,400 results! I started to read some of them and either the people writing the stories were high on something or this cemetery was really active and we had to go and conduct an investigation. I read one story where the person drove into the cemetery and someone else wrote that the place had hurricane wire around the fence to keep people out. Yet another talked about a huge sign that said "Blood Cemetery" across the entrance.

I did find out, though, that there isn't anything sinister about how the cemetery came to be called Blood Cemetery. There was a Dr. Blood who practiced in the area in the late 1800s. He founded the cemetery and it was named for him. I have read that he was a murderer and he buried some of his victims in the cemetery, but I cannot find anything to support this.

I finally found some good directions to get to the place, but it was hard, since it doesn't have an actual address to conduct a search. The family and I arrived at the cemetery on a nice, sunny and warm day. From what I had read about the property on the Internet, I was expecting a whole lot more than we found.

There is no hurricane wire around the fence. As a matter of fact, there is only a small wrought-iron fence that goes across the front of the cemetery. Both sides of the property are bordered by trees and the back of the cemetery butts up against a small pond. There is a small caretaker's shack at the far right rear. There is no ominous sign that says "Blood Cemetery" anyplace I could see. The cemetery is so small that you can't drive into it. No need to—just park on the street and walk a few feet.

There are houses across the street and they *do* keep an eye on the cemetery, which is understandable. I know this since we were only there for a few minutes when an older man came out of his house and to the fence in front of the cemetery to ask us what we were doing there. I told him that we were ghost hunters and just checking the place out. He gave me that "are you serious?" look and said a few things I couldn't hear as he walked back to his house.

I did walk around the cemetery and found the tombstones for the Blood family. It looks like his whole family was buried there. There was a big, old tree almost in the middle of the property. You could feel some weird feelings coming off this tree—and this was in broad daylight. (Imagine what kind of feelings you could get at night!) Even though we were only there for a short time, we decided it was worth gathering a team together and conducting a nighttime investigation.

Somewhere in conversations with my mom, I must have told her that we were going to investigate the cemetery. She e-mailed me to say that she'd talked to my aunt, who works for Clinton County police dispatch, and my aunt told her that whenever I was going to be at the cemetery, to let her know and she would tell the other dispatchers and the officers. Also, if any of the people who lived by the cemetery called the police, they would let them know that we had permission to be on site. (I guess it helps to know people in high places!)

We set a date to investigate the cemetery and assembled a team. I also let my aunt know of our plans. Since some of the team didn't know where the cemetery was, we met in Dewitt and formed a caravan to the cemetery.

THE INVESTIGATION

The night was cloudy and warm, but there was no rain in the forecast. We parked in front of the cemetery and carried what little equipment we would need with us. Walking around the perimeter of the property, we took some photos. Conducting a walkthrough when you first get to a location serves two purposes. The first is that it gives the spirits a chance to know your true intentions, and, secondly, it gives you a chance to see and feel where the activity might be for the evening.

There were two areas where we felt there would be the most activity. The first was the big tree in the middle of the property and the other was the area near the caretaker's shack.

A COLD SPOT AND ORB

Dan and Patrick took the tape recorder and set up near the big tree. The rest of us spread out around the cemetery. We were only there for a few minutes when Patrick came over to me to report that they were already getting good pictures and that there was a cold spot right near the big tree. He said that the

INVESTIGATIVE NOTE

Some groups assign areas and you are assigned to a location for a set amount of time; then you switch. We are old-school and prefer the free-roam method. Basically, everyone goes where they want and takes a piece of equipment with them. What they do, is up to them. Some people will conduct electronic voice phenomenon, or EVP, sessions, while some will just take pictures. We find that this method of investigating works the best for our group. But just because this works for us, doesn't necessarily mean that it will work best for all groups.

There is a big orb near the tree. I asked if the spirit wanted to be in the picture.

cold spot followed them as they moved around the tree, but it always stayed right behind them.

Patrick advised that if anything else happened, he would let me know. With that, he went over and rejoined Dan near the tree. I was close to the caretaker's shack when I felt a cold spot, too. This one wasn't moving, but it stayed stationary between a tree and a few tombstones. I told the spirits that I was going to take a photograph and, if they wanted their picture taken, to stand in front of me when I took it. I counted to three and snapped a picture. Right near the tree and near the tombstones, right where I had felt the cold spot, was a nice, bright orb.

I will admit that the orb looks like it could be a bright, full moon; but, if you remember, the night was cloudy and the moon wasn't visible. Additionally, there was no way that this could be a bug, either—it was too big to be an insect flying by or on the lens. I thanked the spirit for letting me take its picture.

RED EYES

Patrick came back over and said that, in one of the pictures they took by the big tree, there was a pair of red eyes near a tombstone looking back at them. He said that he and Dan had spent the whole time by the tree because they felt a lot of energy there and showed me the picture of the red eyes. I will admit that it did look like two red eyes were looking back at them.

Since we were out in the country, I asked Patrick if the red eyes could have been from a deer or some other kind of wildlife. He didn't think so, since they didn't see or hear any animals when they took the photograph. Even if the picture was an animal, you would still see the body in the photo and, in this picture, all you see are the red eyes.

I asked Patrick to take me to the spot where he took the picture and we walked to a place just south of the big tree, where he pointed toward two small tombstones about twenty feet from us. We took another picture as a control shot, but it didn't show the eyes—or anything else, for that matter.

As we were standing there, however, we heard what sounded like growling and something scratching the tombstones where the two red eyes had been. We both glanced at each other with a look that said, "What the hell was that?" As we walked toward the tombstones, we could still hear the growling and scratching. We were no more than six feet from the graves when we both saw two red eyes peeking around the tombstone, about five feet off the ground. Then we heard something scurry away from us. We gave chase, but we couldn't see or catch up to whatever it was. I don't know to this day what it was that we chased. Yes, it might have been an animal. But usually, if an animal sees or smells humans, it will avoid the area.

This thing was seen twice in the cemetery that night and, except for it running away from us when we approached it, didn't seen scared of us whatsoever. Was it the same thing from the stories told years prior? Is there something really living in this cemetery? Your guess is as good as ours. Either way, it makes for a good story.

Nothing else happened to us the rest of the night. We didn't hear anything else, nor did we see those red eyes again. Again, we thanked the spirits for letting us into their cemetery and asked them to please not follow us home.

We all got into our cars and went our separate ways. To the best of my knowledge, no one brought anything home with them that night.

We haven't been back to the cemetery since that visit. I wish I could say it was because of what happened and that we were too scared to go back. That would make for a good story, too, and maybe add to the urban legend of the cemetery. But the truth is, we have just been too busy helping other people to make a return visit.

Would I like to go back to the cemetery? Hell yeah, I would! I feel like we have unfinished business with whatever it was behind those red eyes. I would like to be the one who finally solves the mystery of Blood Cemetery. Stay tuned!

ELY HIGHWAY CEMETERY

Near the town where I grew up is a small cemetery that I have driven by at least a thousand times over the years. Until I got involved in ghost hunting, I never gave the place a second thought. Once we started our paranormal group and were looking for places to investigate, this cemetery was a logical choice. When Brenda and I decided that we would investigate it, we asked my cousin Marc (one of our first group members) to join us. We set a date for the upcoming Saturday because there was going to be a full moon that night.

Ely Highway Cemetery is divided up into two sections. There is a newer portion on the left side that still has plenty of open spaces for future burials. The older section is on the right side and still has a few open spaces, but not too many. Some of the tombstones there date back to the early 1900s.

Special Note: In the older section sits a small mausoleum. We have been back to the cemetery a few times to just look around and they have put a lock on the front door of the mausoleum. When we conducted our investigation, there wasn't a lock and the mausoleum was open so you could go inside. This may no longer be the case.

THE INVESTIGATION

It was early October when we investigated and there were leaves on the ground. The night was unseasonably warm and there was a nice, full moon high in the sky. It was the kind of moon that gives you enough light that you can see pretty well without the need for a flashlight—but also the kind of moon where light would cast shadows among the tombstones.

I should also mention that this cemetery is in the middle of a more rural area. There is a house across the street, one about a half-mile to the south, and the next closest house is about a mile to the east. When you are in this cemetery at night, it gets really dark.

There are two driveways into the cemetery: a driveway that takes you into the new section and a driveway that takes you into the older section. We took the driveway to the older section and parked right in front of the mausoleum, so the front of the truck was facing the street and the back was facing the mausoleum.

We all got out of the truck and loaded film into the cameras. (Yes, we were still using film back in those days, but we did have a digital camera that night also.) As we usually do in cemeteries, we walked around to get a feeling for the place. It didn't take long for something to happen.

THE COLD SPOT

Marc and I were two sections over from the mausoleum, while Brenda stayed near the truck, and we were making our way to the tombstones near the road when we both felt a cold spot near a row of tombstones. It was a warm night, so the cold spot was easily detectable. It spread out around three tombstones in any direction.

We started taking pictures and, in one of the pictures, there was a good example of ectoplasmic mist—most ghost hunters simply call it "mist." Mists looks like your breath on a cold day or, if you are a smoker, smoke from a cigarette. Mist can be concentrated or barely visible. It all depends on how many

We felt a cold spot near this tombstone and I took this picture. There is ectoplasmic mist in the photo.

21

spirits are in the mist and how much energy is available for them to use. The mist that we saw in the photo from the digital camera was transparent, as you could see things through and behind it. That means that the spirit or spirits in the mist either didn't have enough energy to fully form or we'd just caught the mist as it was starting to form. If the timing was right, we might have caught an apparition on the camera that night.

Just as quickly as we felt it, the cold spot was gone. We walked around the tombstones, but there was no trace of the cold air that had been there moments before. I thanked the spirits for letting us take their picture and we continued on towards the road.

Near the road is a line of pretty impressive tombstones. They are all shapes and sizes, most of them being easily over seven feet tall, and a couple of them we couldn't even begin to describe. We could hear voices from the house across the street—I assumed it was from the TV—and the chorus of insects that were starting to come awake and were talking to each other.

Marc and I were taking pictures of the tombstones when we noticed that the lights in the house went out. It looked like the people there had gone to bed. The only sounds we could hear now were the insects and the occasional car driving down County Line Road.

LAUGHING

I went four tombstones down the line and Marc stood firm where he was. It was near the two tombstones, between Marc and myself, where we suddenly heard what sounded like a giggle or laughter. I couldn't tell if it was a man or woman's voice, but I was sure that I heard something. I immediately looked at Marc and he was already looking at me, his eyes wide with excitement.

"Did you hear that?" Marc asked me.

"Did I hear what?" I responded.

"I heard someone laugh, unless it was you."

"Nope, it wasn't me. Was it you?"

Marc laughed, "Wasn't me, bro. But I know that I heard something."

I said, "I heard something also."

We went to the area where we'd heard the laughter. There was nothing we could find that could have made a noise like that. We use two-way radios when we are in large areas—this makes it easier to communicate with each other and it saves us from yelling over wide areas. I radioed Brenda and asked her where she was.

*I took this picture when I heard laughter near
the road. There are two orbs visible.*

"I am sitting in the truck," Brenda said over the radio. "Why, what's going on?"

I told her what we heard and I was checking her location, so we could rule out that what we'd heard wasn't her. I told her that we would get back with her if anything else happened.

As we were standing there talking about what we'd heard, the same laughter was again heard, but this time it was in front of us, one row of tombstones away. We quickly went to where the laughter came from, but again we couldn't see anything. I looked over to the house and all the lights were still off. I don't think that the laughter was coming from the house.

We'd heard the laughter again and, this time, it was closer to the road—and we were only two rows of tombstones away from it. I quickly took a picture and, this time, there was an orb directly in front of us. It looked like we'd found the source of the laughter.

I took ten more pictures, but nothing showed up in those. We stood in the same spot for ten minutes waiting for the laughter to return, but it never did.

I believe the spirit was having fun with us and it finally got tired and moved someplace else.

Marc and I went back to the truck and told Brenda what had happened. She wanted to check out a few areas in the cemetery and asked one of us to take her. Marc said that he would while I took the chance to go into the mausoleum and see what I could find there. They went off in the direction of the new section of the cemetery and I grabbed the video camera, a tripod, and the digital camera and headed off to the mausoleum.

THE MAUSOLEUM

I opened the front door of the mausoleum and walked in. I placed the tripod and video camera on the floor just inside the front door. The mausoleum was fairly small inside. There was maybe a ten-foot entryway that was just an open area with nothing of note in it. Past that ten feet, on both sides of the mausoleum, were the places where the remains of people that had passed rested in eternal sleep.

The mausoleum was a good sixty to seventy feet long by maybe thirty feet wide. The floor was tiled and my tennis shoes made a squeaking sound as I walked around the interior. The place was dark, except for the light coming from the outside through the open front door, and I couldn't find a light switch anywhere.

Of course, I wouldn't want to turn on any lights because that would change the whole atmosphere. Also, you get better results if you take photos or video in the dark. And there is a popular saying among us ghost hunters: "Ghost Hunters Do It In the Dark."

I walked over to the front door and closed it until I could hear the latch click. Keeping my hand on the door knob, I made an open and close movement with my arm. The door didn't budge. This told me that the door was closed completely and that there was no way that it could swing open on its own. This was important because if the door opened on its own, it meant one of two things: either Marc or Brenda was coming into the mausoleum, or a spirit opened the door to either come in or get out—I wanted to be taking pictures if the latter happened.

With the front door closed, it got really dark in the mausoleum! I didn't notice this with the front door open, but there were a row of windows at the end of the mausoleum. These windows were at the very top of the mausoleum and the light from the outside hit right about in the entryway area.

I walked over and grabbed the tripod, setting it up so the legs were hitting the wall just to the right of the front door. I screwed the plate of the tripod to the bottom of the video camera and set the video camera on the tripod, pointing the camera towards the end of the mausoleum. Then I hit the record button. I told the spirits that the camera would not hurt them and that it was only there to record them and catch their image on film, if they so wanted.

INVESTIGATIVE NOTE

If you are conducting an investigation in an outdoor location, make sure that all of the batteries you bring with you for your equipment are fully charged. There is nothing worse than having batteries fail after only an hour because you forgot to charge them beforehand.

I took the digital camera out of my pocket and started taking pictures, but did not get good results. Starting to walk to the end of the mausoleum, I could hear my shoes making a squeaking sound with each footstep and, in the quiet of the mausoleum, the sound echoed off the walls.

As I neared the far wall I stopped, but I heard two more footsteps, or in this case squeaks, behind me! I immediately turned around, fully expecting to see either Marc or Brenda behind me, but there was no one there! I was alone in the mausoleum. I started taking pictures all over the room to see if I could get whoever was in there with me on the digital camera.

I took twenty pictures in a two-minute period and I didn't see anything on the digital camera. So I started thinking about what could have caused the sound I'd heard. Could have it been a loose tile on the floor? Maybe it was the sound of my own footsteps that somehow echoed off the walls and I just *thought* that I had heard the extra footsteps?

I decided there was only one way to settle this. I would walk back to the front of the mausoleum and then retrace my steps to where I'd heard the extra footsteps behind me. If it happened again, then it probably was a loose floor tile or an echo. But if I retraced my footsteps and, this time, I didn't hear any extra ones...well, I guess that would prove that I wasn't alone in the mausoleum.

I walked back to the front of the mausoleum and stopped...no extra footsteps were heard on the way back. I turned and retraced my steps to the far end of the mausoleum and when I stopped, there were no extra footsteps behind me! That pretty much ruled out loose floor tiles and that the extra footsteps were caused by an echo. So, I wasn't alone in the mausoleum. And, you know what? It didn't bother me one bit.

I walked around the mausoleum a bit longer taking some pictures, but again I didn't get anything on the digital camera. It might be worth noting, too, that the time I was walking around, I didn't hear the extra footsteps. I figured that nothing else was going to happen, so I walked back to the front of the mausoleum and turned off the video camera. I kept it on the tripod in case I needed to use it later on in the cemetery. Opening the door to the mausoleum, I paused, then turned to face the empty building and I thanked the spirits for allowing me in their home. I turned and closed the door behind me.

A few days later, when I was watching the video from the camera that I'd had with me in the mausoleum, I was fortunate enough to be in view of the video camera when I'd stopped and heard the extra footsteps. You can see and hear me walking away from the camera. I then stop and you hear the two extra footsteps. At the exact moment that you hear the two extra footsteps, a very bright orb materializes directly a few feet behind me. The orb then veers off to the left and it is gone.

What is interesting is that the orb appears when you hear the two extra footsteps and as soon as the orb disappears, the footsteps stop. Even without a physical body, the spirit was able to make footstep sounds.

When I came out of the mausoleum, I could see a flashlight over in the new section. Brenda and Marc were still there, so I took the opportunity to put the tripod and video camera back in the truck. I also loaded some film in the 35mm camera and looked at the pictures on the digital camera from the mausoleum while I waited for them to return.

Brenda's Scare

It was getting to be close to 10 p.m. and, at that time of year, it was pitch dark. I wasn't ready to leave yet and I asked Brenda and Marc if they wanted to stay for a little while longer. They both said they would, but Brenda was done investigating and advised that she would stay in the truck while Marc and I went out.

I took the digital camera and a flashlight and Marc took his video camera and a flashlight. I grabbed a two-way radio and did a radio check. Brenda could hear me fine. She assumed her position in the front seat and Marc and I went off into the cemetery.

We just walked around taking pictures and video, starting in the new section and working our way over into the older part of the cemetery. After half an hour, I'd used up the film in the camera and we talked about going back to the truck and loading more film so we could take some more pictures. But before we could start back, Brenda came on the two way radio.

"Where are you guys at?"

"We are over by the road, near the big tombstones," I responded. "Why?"

"I want to leave now," came Brenda's answer.

I looked at Marc and he gave me this puzzled look.

"But we aren't ready to leave yet," I said.

"I want to leave right now!" Brenda said sternly.

"Okay," I said.

We started walking back to the truck and I will admit that I was a little aggravated. When we got to the truck, Brenda was still in the front seat. We put the equipment in the cases and closed the tailgate. Marc and I got into the truck and we drove out of the cemetery, heading back to town.

We dropped Marc off and drove the two blocks to my mom's house to pick up the kids. We had an hour drive back to our home and I asked Brenda why she was in such a hurry to get out of the cemetery. I only wished that she would have told me why while we were still *in* the cemetery—not after we had left. Here was her reason for leaving:

> I was sitting in the truck and I could see your flashlights off in the distance. I was doing fine until I heard leaves rustling behind the truck. It was the sound that someone makes when they are walking through leaves that have fallen on the ground. As soon as I looked back behind the truck to see who it was, the sound stopped.
>
> I could tell that it wasn't any small animal making this sound. It could have been a deer, but it sounded much bigger. I was getting a little freaked out at this point.
>
> I knew it wasn't you guys because I saw your flashlights near the road. But if it wasn't you two, then who was it? Of course your mind starts thinking all of these crazy thoughts, and you start thinking about every bad horror movie you have ever seen, and the girl is always to first to be killed.
>
> I sat still for a few minutes, but I didn't hear any more sounds coming from behind the truck. Just when I had myself reassured that maybe I was only hearing things, I could hear that "someone was walking through fallen leaves" sound again. But, this time, it was closer to the back of the truck, whereas before the sound was closer to the mausoleum.
>
> I looked back again, expecting the sound to stop, but it continued and the sound came right up beside the passenger side of the truck and stopped right outside my door! There was no way in hell that I was going to look to see if anything was there. I sat perfectly still, waiting for something to happen—like a knock on the window or the door handle to move—but thankfully nothing happened. That's when I called you on the two-way radio and said we had to go.

After she was finished telling the story, I told her that what happened to her was cool and I'd wished it had happened to me instead. We made it home okay and, as far as I know, we didn't bring anything home with us. We still pass by the cemetery when we visit my mom and, one day, we will go there at night and investigate again. Maybe our visitors will return to say "hi!"

LOVEJOY CEMETERY

We were asked to conduct an investigation as a fundraiser for a local business in conjunction with the local Railroad Days. We had the day and time for the event, but not the place and were asked if we knew of a place that was haunted where we could investigate. A local cemetery came to mind and we asked and received permission to conduct a late-night investigation.

The cemetery is named Lovejoy and we had been to this one before. A few years prior, a friend of ours suggested that we make a visit there—he had heard rumors for years that the place was haunted.

AN EARLIER INVESTIGATION

As chance would have it, a few weeks after he told us about the cemetery, we were conducting a house investigation in the area and the decision was made to visit Lovejoy after we were finished at the home. We arrived at the cemetery at around midnight. There are two driveways off the main road. The first one is the exit, so we went to the second driveway and turned in. There is only one path through the grounds, so we followed it back around to the road and parked the vehicles.

There were four vehicles and five members of the group that made the visit that night. Four of them went off into the cemetery and I went to a hill that took you to the main part of the grounds. The hill is steep and I started to make my way up to some tombstones at the top. I didn't make it more than a few feet when I started to hear whispers.

WHISPERING

The whispers were coming from my direct left. The closest house is a few miles away and I could hear the other members of the group on the other side of the cemetery. The voices were too close to be anyone in the group. I couldn't make out what was being said, but I believe there were only two different voices that I could make out. It sounded like a man and woman having a conversation.

I stood still, listening to the voices. I could hear them for only a few minutes; then they started to fade away, until they were gone. Of course, I didn't have my recorder going because, quite honestly, I didn't expect this much activity.

FOOTSTEPS

I continued up the hill and, when I was just about to reach the top, I stopped dead in my tracks and listened. I could hear footsteps from just over the hill and they were coming straight for me! This wasn't like the previous cemetery, where you could hear the footsteps because of the fallen leaves on the ground. This time there were no leaves and you could hear the footsteps in the grass because they were so damn heavy. Whatever was making these footsteps was either a big person or they just stepped down heavy when they walked. Either way, I was about to find out.

I stood just short of the crest of the hill and waited to see who was making the footsteps. I had my digital camera ready, just in case. But I never found out who was making those footsteps. They came just short of my sight of view and stopped! I listened intently, but there was no movement and no more footsteps. I climbed the ten or so feet to stand on the top of the hill. I could see the other members over by the fence line on the other side of the cemetery. There was no way that it could have been one of them making the footsteps—or the whispers, for that matter. They didn't have enough time to go from where I was to where I saw them in such a short amount of time. I would have heard them if they would have tried.

I snapped a few pictures, but didn't get anything. Meeting up with the other members, I told them what happened. They all reported a quiet time, with nothing happening during their investigation. Everyone had a long drive back home, so we all decided to call it a night. We thanked the spirits for an interesting night and got in our vehicles and left.

FUNDRAISING INVESTIGATIONS

Just from what had happened to the group on our previous visit to the cemetery, I knew that this would be a good place to host an investigation for a fundraiser. This time around the cemetery didn't disappoint, either!

HISTORIC SIGNIFICANCE

Lovejoy Cemetery does have some history behind it. On August 6, 1903, The Great Wallace Brothers Circus Train Disaster occurred in the city of Durand.

According to Historic Views of Owosso and Corunna Michigan's website: www.shiawasseehistory.com/circus.html:

> At 8:30 p.m., at the Grand Trunk railroad yards in Durand, two separate trains of the Wallace Brothers shows met in a rear end collision that resulted in the death of 23 people and twice as many were injured.
>
> Several animals were killed including an Arabian horse, 3 camels, one Great Dane and an elephant named Maud. The accident occurred as the engine of the second train smashed into several cars of the first. The animals were buried at this location.
>
> The first train had pulled into Durand from Charlotte en route to Lapeer. It stopped at the west end of the yards on the main track. A red light was put out to signal the second train. The engineer saw the light and attempted to stop his train, but the air brakes failed and the engine crashed into the rear of the front train with "terrific force."

Ten bodies were unclaimed and were buried in Lovejoy Cemetery. Of this number, one of the bodies was claimed, taken up, and removed to New York state. Nine board signs were prominent in the cemetery over each of the unknown victims.

There is a monument in Lovejoy Cemetery dedicated to the train wreck. It reads:

> In Memory of the Unknown Dead Who Lost Their Lives in the RAILROAD WRECK of the GREAT WALLACE SHOWS August 6, 1903.

If you enter the second driveway into the cemetery, coming from the south, the monument is located about fifty feet in and on your left.

We decided that we would have two investigations at Lovejoy at night for the fundraiser. The first one would be from 10 p.m to midnight and the other would run from 1 a.m. to 3 a.m. When the night finally came, we met at a local business to talk a little about the investigations. The people who paid to be with us had no idea where the investigations were going to be held until we got ready to head out to the cemetery. The announcement that the investigations were going to be at a local cemetery at night drew mostly cheers. A few moans could also be heard.

Monument in the cemetery giving information
about the circus train accident.

THE FIRST INVESTIGATION

We were the lead vehicle for the caravan to the cemetery and seven other cars followed us. Arriving at the cemetery a little after 10 p.m., we took the second driveway into the cemetery, driving all the way around until we were a few feet from the road. All of the cars parked behind us on the driveway.

Getting out of our SUV, we waited for the others to join us. We told them what to expect from the investigation and to be alert, because anything could happen at a known-haunted location. We also mentioned to them that since this was an outdoor investigation, they could expect to be bothered by insects and, if they heard any noises, to make sure first that the sounds were not caused by insects or animals that might be close to them. They were advised that they had free roam of the cemetery, but to watch out for the steep hill.

We said the opening prayer—we say this for protection before the investigation starts—then asked if there were any questions. There were none, so we told the group that they were more than welcome to hook up with one of our members or they could go investigate on their own. Most of the people came with friends, so they headed off on their own, but some did pair up with our members. I basically roamed the cemetery and answered any questions that people had.

During this first investigation of the night, there was some minor activity reported near the northeast corner of the cemetery. Some of our guests felt a cold spot around one of the tombstones. When they took a picture, they got an orb near the spot where they felt the cold. Another group of people thought they heard voices around the same area. They couldn't be sure if the voices were from the living or dead.

THE FLASHING LIGHT

We got a report from one of the groups that they were seeing a flashing light near the infant section of the cemetery. (To be honest with you, this section was sad to see. Some of the infants only lived for a few days before they passed. I couldn't even imagine the kind of grief that the parents would have felt to lose a child.) ...Back to the flashing lights that people were seeing. The light was a few feet off the ground, but didn't move. They said it didn't seem to follow any pattern when viewed, but just seemed to blink randomly. I asked them to show me where the light was and was taken to the spot where a group of four people were standing in the area. They pointed to a tree—I would say was no more than fifty feet away from where we were standing.

I was instructed to: "Look just to the right of the tree and you will see a light flash—and it isn't a lightning bug. This light is much bigger and flashes different colors."

While we were waiting for the light to make an appearance, I asked someone from the group why we were standing so far away from the light and why someone didn't investigate further. One young man turned and looked me straight in the eye and told me, "That's your job. This s**t scares me, but I have an interest." The rest in the group nodded their approval to his answer.

I laughed at his answer. Not because I was laughing at him, but rather his truthful reply. Sure enough, after a few minutes, a bright light quickly flashed and then was gone.

"See…we weren't lying. You did see it, right?" someone excitedly asked me.

"Yeah, I saw it," I responded. "Let's see what this light is."

I started walking towards the tree to where the light was seen, the group a few steps behind me. A few feet to the right and behind the tree was the source of the light. A few feet off the ground was one of the lights that people put in cemeteries near a loved one's tombstone. (If you are ever in a cemetery after dark, you will know what I am talking about. There are all kinds: some are different colors, some blink, while some are steady and of different intensities.)

This light had a black frame, with clear glass covering the light. Because of the black frame and the darkness, the frame could not be seen—only the light. From a distance, the light looked like it was floating in the air.

"There is your mysterious light," I said, pointing.

Someone in the group laughed and said, "I feel foolish."

I told them, "You have nothing to feel foolish about. You saw something you couldn't explain and told someone about it. There is nothing wrong with that."

This little light had some serious problems, though. Either the battery was going out or the light had a short. It was after dark and the light should have been on. Instead, it was flashing on and off randomly. Just the short time we were standing there, it flashed on and off three times and in quick succession. By my count, three different colors: red, green, and white.

❧ CONTACT ❧

With this little excitement over, the group went on their way and I continued on in the cemetery. There was a place near the back corner that I'd picked up on earlier in the investigation and I wanted to go back to see if I could find something there. I had only been in the area for a few minutes when I started to get a buzzing in my right ear. (This can happen in either of my ears, and it usually means that a spirit is trying to talk to me.) I asked the spirit a few questions in my mind and waited for a response. I wasn't hearing anything from the spirit and I thought this odd, since *it* was the one that started "talking" to me. I told the spirit I had to leave and thanked it for at least attempting to communicate with me.

I took this picture of an orb when I heard footsteps in front of me. Notice that this photo has a date stamp. A date/time stamp is a good thing to place on photographs when conducting investigations. This way, you know precisely when the picture was taken and you can reference it to any events that might occur.

I turned to leave when I heard what sounded like footsteps in front of me. I took a quick picture and looked at the digital camera. Right in front of me was a very bright orb. Could this be the spirit that was trying to make contact with me? I thanked the spirit for letting me take its picture and started back towards the cars.

❦ A MILITARY GHOST ❧

This investigation was nearing an end, so we started gathering the participants and told them to meet us at the vehicles to compare notes. When everyone was present, I asked if anyone had experienced anything. Other than the flashing light and hearing the odd noise, there was no reported activity. I quickly said our closing prayer and told the group that I'd heard footsteps in front of me and when I'd taken a picture there was a nice, bright orb just in front of me. I told them that Brenda had an experience and she stepped in front of the group to tell them what happened:

> I was standing with some people at the top of the hill near the center of the cemetery; we were standing near some tombstones and were talking about nothing in particular. I looked over and saw this man standing just a few feet from me. He was looking right at me and he had his arms crossed. The thing that struck me was that he was wearing what looked to be a military uniform—if I had to guess, I would have to say that it was a Navy uniform. [Brenda described what he looked like.] I looked away for a few seconds and, when I looked back, he was gone. I quickly looked around the area to see where he had gone to. He couldn't have gone far because I only turned away for a few seconds, but I could not find him.
>
> As I look at you guys, no one is dressed like the man that I saw. Now I am not saying that I saw a ghost, but I have no other explanation for what I saw.

With that, Brenda slipped back into the group and I stepped forward to thank the people for coming and where they could talk with us if needed.

We left the cemetery and went back to the local business handling the fundraiser. One of the people from the first investigation met us in the parking lot to thank us and to mention that she enjoyed herself.

"I didn't want to say anything there," she began, "because I didn't want people to think that I was weird, but I think I know who the man in uniform was who was back at the cemetery."

"First off, you are not weird. Second, who do you think the man was?" I asked.

"I think it was my father! He served in the Navy, and is buried at Lovejoy. Your wife described him to a 'T'. I was with the group that was with your wife and we were standing in the military section of Lovejoy when she saw him!"

She went on to tell me that it confirmed her feelings that he was around her sometimes.

THE SECOND INVESTIGATION

Within a few minutes, the attendees of the second investigation started arriving. When we told this group that the "mystery" location was Lovejoy Cemetery, there was a smattering of clapping. We told them what to expect at the cemetery and some of the things that had happened at the first investigation.

INVESTIGATIVE NOTE

There is a free app that can be downloaded to your phone to help with ghost investigations. The one we use is called Ghost Radar. It will give you either spoken words or you can switch to a radar screen that will show you where spirits are in reference to where you are standing.

In radar mode, the spirits will "appear" as colored blips on the screen. The colors of the blips are an indication of signal strength. Red indicates the signal is strongest. Yellow is a little weaker signal than red. Green is a little weaker signal than yellow. Finally, blue indicates a very weak signal.

Whether or not you believe in these apps is entirely up to you. However, we have had success in using these on our investigations.

Again, the people followed us to Lovejoy. As in the first investigation, we had them park their cars behind ours on the drive. We waited for everyone to join us in front of the tombstones that were at the corner nearest the cars. After saying the opening prayer, we retrieved some of the equipment from our SUV.

I briefly pointed out some of the "hot spots" from the earlier investigation in the cemetery, and then gave them the same instructions for investigating.

Most of the people went off on their own, while a few brave souls paired up with members from our group. A group of three teenagers had downloaded the app and were using it to "chase" down the spirits that were in the cemetery that night. Another group—this one made up of adults—was walking around the cemetery using the app to try to receive words spoken by the spirits.

The second investigation turned out to be quiet, which happens from time to time. (You have to realize that there isn't an activity switch that you can turn on to make things happen for you. There are a lot of outside factors that influence the spirits and what they can or can't do.)

I did have an experience towards the end of the investigation. We had been there for almost two and a half hours and we only had another half-hour left before we had to leave. I was standing near the edge at the top of the hill. Down below me, to my right—a drop of at least twelve feet—were five tombstones. Right in front of me and to my left were a couple of smaller tombstones.

A Woman in White

I had the MEL EMF meter (a brand of electromagnetic frequency detection equipment) with me and I got two quick spikes that registered a 5.6 and 6.3 milligauss, respectively. That meant that there were possibly spirits within a

Bright orb where I saw a woman in white going past.

short distance of me. At that exact time, I also felt a very strong, cold area just in front and to the left. As I usually do at cemetery investigations when I feel something or the equipment indicates possible spirits in the area, I looked down at the nearest tombstone and read the name. I then ask the spirit, who is identified by the name on the tombstone, if they want to talk to us or give us a message. I instruct them to talk into the red light on the recorder if they want to speak.

I waited for a few seconds for a reply; then I rewound the recorder and hit play to see if I'd captured any EVP. I didn't hear anything on the recorder, so I looked down at another tombstone to try a different name to hopefully get a response.

As I was looking down at the tombstone, out of the corner of my eye, I saw a white streak that was moving to the left of me. I looked up and, for a split second, I saw a woman in a long, white dress running past me; then, just as quickly, she was gone. She had simply vanished. From the short time I saw her, all I could see was that she had brown hair. I immediately took a picture and in the picture there is a bright orb with some white-colored "things" around it. Could this be the woman in white that I saw? I can't say for sure, but I like the odds.

I took a couple more pictures of the area, but they came out without anything odd in them. I thanked the "woman in white" for allowing me to see her, albeit quickly. With that, our time was up and we needed to be out of the cemetery.

We would love to make a return visit to Lovejoy Cemetery sometime soon. Maybe on our next visit the man in uniform or the lady in white will come back and say "hi" to us again. Lovejoy Cemetery is an active cemetery and I don't mean just for the living.

PURPLE ROSE THEATER

In the summer of 2008, we were looking for a place to conduct an investigation and, while Brenda was looking on the Internet, she came across the Purple Rose Theater. She quickly fired off an e-mail to the address given on the website.

To be honest, I wasn't expecting to hear back from the Purple Rose. You see, some places don't want to be known as being haunted for fear that it will keep customers away or attract ghost hunters (like us!) and they don't want to deal with them. Other places, however, embrace the fact that they have a spirit or two hanging around the place.

After a few days, we received an e-mail from the Purple Rose Theater saying that they would be interested in allowing us to do an investigation at their establishment. Brenda called to set up a date and time for the investigation.

As luck would have it, they were doing a play about an apartment that was haunted. I forgot the actual name of the play but it was something like "Apartment 3A." They asked if the actors in the play could be there for the investigation to observe and ask questions. Some of our investigations have happened because we were in the right place at the right time. Timing is everything.

According to the theater website:

> Founded in 1991 by acclaimed actor and Chelsea native Jeff Daniels, The Purple Rose Theatre Company is a creative home for theatre artists to define our collective Midwestern voice. It is a place for emerging talent and seasoned professionals to learn more about and to practice their craft; a place for patrons of the arts to laugh, cry, and perhaps even learn something new.
>
> In the early 1900s, the building that houses our "Garage Theatre" was a used car and bus garage owned by Jeff Daniels' grandfather. In 1989, the building was purchased and renovated by Mr. Daniels and later donated to the Purple Rose.

We arrived at the back of the theater on the night of the investigation. The company manager, Amy invited us into the building. Standing in the actors' lounge, we found a TV, couch, some chairs, and a small kitchen. Also available to the actors were a laundry room and showers. There were a few actors milling around and Amy introduced us to Artistic Director Guy Sanville, who was directing the haunted apartment play. (He has directed over thirty plays at the theater.)

FUN FACTS

We looked Guy Sanville up at the Internet Movie Database (IMDB) website (www.imdb.com) after we did the investigation and he has appeared in numerous films, including one with Jeff Daniels in 2002, *Super Sucker.* Guy played the part of Leonard and dressed in drag in one scene during the movie. It was funny to have seen Guy at the theater that night on a serious investigation, then to see him later dressed as a woman during a movie.

After the introductions were over, Guy invited us to share dinner with the group. During that time, the actors, and even Guy himself, asked us questions about what we did, the equipment we used, and our most interesting cases. They had some good questions and we enjoyed answering them. Guy told us that he would take us on a tour of the building and then we would be able to start the investigation, having full access to the building.

THE THEATER TOUR

For the tour, we took out our EMF meters, digital thermometers, a couple of tape recorders, video cameras, and digital cameras.

INVESTIGATIVE NOTE

In a private home or business, we take temperature and EMF readings of every room to be used as baseline readings. So, let's say that during an investigation we get a high EMF reading in a certain area; we can look back at the baseline readings and see what the readings were before the investigation started. If we'd recorded high EMF readings at the start and continued to get high EMF readings during the investigation, then we would look for the cause of these high readings. But if we had no EMF readings and during the investigation we got an EMF spike in an area, it could mean a spirit is in the area.

Guy started us out in the office area of the building. We went from office to office and he told us whose office we were visiting and what that person did. We took base readings, but we didn't get any spikes either for temperature nor EMF. The last office we went to belonged to Jeff Daniels. (I thought his office would be bigger!)

FUN FACTS

As soon as you walk into the office of Jeff Daniels, there are two chairs from the old Tiger Stadium against the left wall. Directly above these chairs is a nicely framed picture of said stadium. His desk is straight ahead and against the right wall are book shelves. Leaning up against his desk is an acoustic guitar and there are pictures of him with numerous movie stars on the walls.

❧ EMF SPIKE AND ORB ☙

Photo of an orb where we were getting high EMF readings. Courtesy of Brenda Mikulka.

The next area we went to was the front lobby/ticket window area. This area was pretty big and it gave us room to move around a little without bumping into each other. Halfway down the front lobby, past the doors to get into the actual theater, we recorded our first EMF spike of the evening. Brenda took a picture where we were getting the spike and there was a bright orb right in that same area. I showed Guy and some of the actors the picture and Guy wanted to know why we thought that the light was a spirit. I told Guy that since our EMF meter went off and there was an orb in the area, it probably wasn't dust or pollen. I went on to explain that an orb is another form in which we can see a spirit. He seemed to accept this and when I showed the picture to the actors, they all seemed to be impressed with it.

The next place we toured was the actual theater itself. It was a fairly good-sized theater with the stage in the middle of the room and seats on risers on three sides. The seats were set up like movie-theater seating, so there wasn't a bad seat in the house. Guy asked us to not go onto the stage because there were props from the current play there and he didn't want anyone to hurt themselves.

INVESTIGATIVE NOTE

Another good reason for a tour of a building before beginning is to highlight any dangers or areas that might cause problems during the investigation. Remember, you don't know the building as well as the owners do.

We went backstage next. It had the usual things one might expect: ladders, props, lighting, etc. There was a very small passageway that ran behind the stage to the dressing rooms. This was how the actors could change clothes so quickly and still get back on stage before their next lines. This is also where I first made contact with George. He was a friendly old spirit that roamed the theater. (I will have more on him later in the chapter.)

Next on the tour was the basement. It looked like any other basement, but this one had some heavy-duty power equipment to make the props and walls for the stage. There were a couple of pieces of clothing hanging on racks that looked like they hadn't been used in years. In one corner were boxes upon boxes of Christmas decorations. From the amount that they had, it would appear the theater was decorated really well for the holidays.

That concluded the tour of the building. We all joined back together in the actors' lounge area to set up a plan of attack for the investigation. The building was big enough that we could break up into teams and not get in each other's way. Some of our members went into the basement, some into the theater, and some stayed in the lounge area. They each took some of the equipment and off they went. I went to the front lobby/ticket window area with a few actors and Guy, and we quickly met up with George and Helen.

GEORGE AND HELEN

George, the spirit, was in his early 60s and the maintenance worker at the building many years ago, before it became the Purple Rose Theater. There had been many reports of people seeing the spirit of an older man in coveralls roaming the building over the years. In my conversation with him, he told me that he had died in the 1920s and has been roaming the building since. When asked why he hadn't crossed over, he told me that he enjoyed the building and especially liked to watch the plays that were put on there. I asked him if we could take his picture and he was agreeable. I told him that we would count to three and then take his picture. We took it and a bright orb was right where George was standing while I was talking to him.

An orb that is a spirit named George who resides in the building. Courtesy of Brenda Mikulka.

While talking to George, the spirit of a little girl made her presence known. She started talking to me, telling me that her name was Helen and that she was nine years old. Her parents used to own the building when it was a car repair garage. She was killed outside in front of the building when a car ran her over. They brought her back inside the building and called for a doctor; but, there wasn't anything that could have been done to save her.

The child went to her own funeral and told me that she liked it. She came back to the building because she had fond memories playing there. Her parents sold the business a few years later, but she stayed and has been there ever since. I asked her the year of her death and she told me 1925. She advised me that she does not see the other spirits in the building with her.

One of the actors said that he was going to go outside to take a smoke break. As he was walking past us to go outside, Helen said to tell him that smoking was bad for him.

I called out to the actor, "Helen has a message for you."

He stopped, "What is the message?"

"Smoking is bad for you!"

Some of the actors at The Purple Rose Theater watching a monitor. Notice the orb watching them.

"I know; tell her thanks for letting me know."

I told him that he just technically did, explaining to the whole group that spirits can hear you when you speak to them. Unless you are a medium, however, you can't usually hear them with your real ears. I asked them to talk to both George and Helen on occasion and they agreed. The actor, I'm afraid, went outside to smoke the cigarette that was bad for him anyway!

Though both George and Helen were most likely still in the building, they pulled back and seemed to leave the area. Guy had said that he felt like someone was watching him when he was backstage. I let him know that George hangs out back there and it was probably him he felt.

I made contact with George a few more times during the night, but Helen didn't make herself known for the rest of the investigation.

Our little group split up and I was the only one left in the hallway. The actors scattered to other parts of the building and Guy went into the theater.

We had set up a video camera in the theater and then ran the cable to a monitor that we put on a cart near some of the seats. Guy was now sitting in front of that monitor, as were two actors, and one of our members was sitting in a seat one row down from the monitor. A picture was taken of that group of people, and there was a bright orb directly behind them. It seemed like the spirit was either watching the people, or was in fact watching the monitor to see what was happening there.

NOISES

The next couple of hours at the Purple Rose were quiet. It almost seemed like someone flipped a switch and all of the activity stopped. None of the teams were reporting any type of occurrence and it was getting to be around three in the morning.

INVESTIGATIVE NOTE

Believe it or not, spirits are curious about new things they might not have seen when they were alive. We have encountered this many times during our investigations. A picture will be taken and there will be an orb either around us or around our equipment.

Some of the members and I decided to just sit in the empty theater to see if anything would happen. We were spread out across the theater. I will admit that, just sitting there, the eyelids were starting to get a little heavy. We hadn't been there too long, though, when we heard a noise coming from the stage area. (We think it was near the stage area, but due to the echo in the empty theater it was hard to say for certain.)

The best way of describing the sound would be to think of something being dragged across a wooden floor. The reason we thought the sound may have come from the stage is because the floor of the theater, except for the stage, is carpeted. We heard the noise for a few seconds and then it stopped.

INVESTIGATIVE NOTE

Anytime you hear a noise on an investigation, the first thing you should do as investigators is to try to find the source and eliminate any man-made causes.

There was no one near the stage at the time, so we did a fast radio check and found that no one was in the backstage area. We all waited in complete silence to see if the noise would repeat. A few minutes later, we all heard the noise again. This time, however, there were three footsteps and then the sliding noise—then complete silence again.

We tried to find any logical explanation for the noises, but we couldn't come up with any. We didn't hear the noises again after that.

A picture of our group in the early morning after our investigation.

It was pushing four in the morning and some of the actors had to leave, since they had to be back in at noon. We decided to make one more sweep of the building and call it a night.

We haven't had the chance to go back to the Purple Rose Theater, but we hope to someday. We had a good time and the people there all made us feel welcome and that was appreciated. If you are looking to see a good play, check out their website and see what is being performed (www.purplerosetheatre.org). You never know what ghostly encounter you might have on your visit!

DURAND UNION STATION

We have done many investigations at the Durand Union Station over the years. Most recently, we were involved in a fundraiser over the course of three weeks. During this time we had some great experiences and one excellent video. Here you will find some of our experiences encountered while not only conducting investigations there, but during a daytime visit that was totally *not* ghost related. These occurrences cover many investigations over the years. Unlike the previous chapters in this book, this one will be presented like a collection of short stories and I will write about the things that happened while in the building over the years.

Specific details about the building are readily available online if you'd like to learn more about the station itself. I *will* tell you that Amtrak still makes stops at the Durand Union Station and the first floor is used as the ticket area for this. I am not sure how many stops or the times that Amtrak visits, but I know that during our time conducting investigations, the Amtrak pulled in around 9:30 p.m. and either dropped off or picked up passengers. The train was only there for a few minutes and then I believe it continues towards Chicago. (Further travel information may be found online, if needed.)

There are people, a.k.a. train watchers, that frequent the Durand Union Station at all times of the day to take photographs or to watch the trains that go by the station. You need to be careful when you are investigating that you don't confuse these people for the spirits.

The Durand Union Station consists of the main building and a separate structure right behind it that is used for luggage. During WWII, the luggage building was also used to store the coffins with the remains of service members killed overseas until they could be loaded onto another train to continue their journeys home.

The main building consists of two floors—three if you include the attic. As you enter the main door, there is a room to your left that is now the gift shop. Back in the day, this was the cafeteria, where hungry travelers could sit and enjoy a meal. To your right is a hallway that takes you to the ticket area. Here, you will find a self-service kiosk where people can buy tickets for the train, and this area is also used as a waiting area. Right off the ticket area is a ladies' rest room that has reports of paranormal activity even to this day.

If you went back to the main stairs, they would take you to the second floor and you would be in a long hallway that runs left to right. To your left, at the end of the hallway, there is a room that was once used as a ballroom. It was divided up into offices, but they took them out years ago and it once again looks how it did years ago. To your right, at the end of the hallway, is the door to the attic. Just before the door to the attic, if you were to look up, you would see a small hatch and, if you had a ladder, you could open the hatch to find yourself in another attic that runs the whole length of the building.

There are a few small offices on either side of the hallway as well as a restroom. On the left side of the hallway is a larger room that is now the Directors Board Room. During our investigations we took over the ballroom. It is in this room where we set up tables and monitors and kept the equipment. We always had at least one person sitting to watch the monitors for any paranormal activity.

THE FIRST INVESTIGATION

The first thing that happened during our first investigation many years ago was experienced near the ticket window on the first floor. A couple of our members were between the ladies' bathroom and the ticket window. One of them saw a shadow come out from the wall, move a few feet into the room, and then go back from where it came. Then it was gone. She couldn't tell if the shadow was male or female; however, guessing by the size of the shadow, she thought it was a man. Not frightened by the shadow, it did catch her off guard because it came out of nowhere.

Let me say that the experiences that I am sharing in this section go beyond just photographs and video, and usually are not recorded documentation. The reason these events were not caught on a video or in a photo is because either the area wasn't covered with a video camera or the person experiencing them didn't have a camera ready to take a picture. Things happen fast sometimes and there isn't always time to snap a picture. Another reason is that we were just not ready. That has happened to us on countless investigations. We are getting better, but sometimes we still miss the occasional orb or two.

Something else happened to us on that same investigation that is worth noting—and it happened to me. I was walking down the hallway to the ticket area when I noticed movement out of the corner of my right eye. I immediately looked that way and saw a black form dash from the far left pillar to the ticket window. The shape was about the size of a woman, even though I didn't see any features. I walked over to where I last saw the black form, but I couldn't see anything.

I figured if the black form was here once, it might make another appearance. I sat down on the bench closest to the ticket window with my back to the wall. From this position I had an unobstructed view from the ticket window to the ladies' restroom on the far left side of the room.

You would be surprised at how many odd noises you hear in an old building in the middle of the night. There would be a creaking sound behind me. Then I would hear another creaking sound over by the ATM. I stopped looking in the directions of the noises after the first ten, simply because my neck was starting to get sore from turning my head so much.

My phone said that it was a little after one in the morning. When I put my phone back down, I looked up and the black form had indeed made another appearance! I watched silently as the form quietly made its way from the ticket window, that was only a few feet from me, towards the ladies' restroom. I watched it enter the restroom; then it was out of my sight.

Getting up from the bench, I quickly moved to the ladies' restroom, which on this first floor is divided into two different sections. As you first enter, I would say that this was once referred to as the sitting room. There is a fireplace, a chair and table, and a little couch where one could lie down or lounge. The connected room is where two sinks and a couple of stalls are located. I swiftly looked in both rooms, but could find no hint of the black form.

People have reported that when they use the stall on the right, as soon as you enter the room, they feel like they are being watched, and there have even been a couple reports where the stall door has opened on its own accord while someone was using the facility.

This first investigation happened a few months before Halloween that year because I remember being asked to do a radio interview with 1240 WJIM, a local radio station in Lansing. I was in the studio and we were talking about ghosts, Halloween, and some other ghost-related things when the DJ asked me about some of the recent investigations that we had done. I mentioned the Durand Union Station and agreed to take questions from listeners. As luck would have it, the first caller was Tammy, our contact for the Station and president of the board back then. She said that there had been recent activity and that the black form had been seen again in the same area where I had seen it. She asked if we would be interested in returning, but this time it could be an all-night investigation if we so desired.

Well, of course.

THE SECOND INVESTIGATION

A couple of things that happened at the second investigation went beyond the norm. The first involved a spirit that was in the ladies' restroom on the first floor. Our friend Linda sensed the spirit and started talking to it. This is what Linda told us:

> I walked into the ladies' restroom on the first floor and immediately sensed that there was a spirit of a woman sitting on the sofa in the sitting room. From the way that she was dressed, I would say that she was from the early 1900s. The spirit told me that she was on a train traveling by herself and that Durand was not her scheduled stop.
>
> The spirit said that she had become ill on the train and the conductor and some of the passengers tried to help her out the best they could. When they arrived in Durand, they removed her from the train and laid her down on the couch. Someone called for a doctor and he arrived a short time later.
>
> The spirit told me that she was feeling sick before she left for her trip, but she didn't want to miss her train because she was going to meet her husband in Detroit. He had gone there to find work and he had finally gotten a job. They were going to have a weekend together before she would return back to their house to pack up their belongings to move there with him.
>
> She'd felt hot and, after the doctor examined her, he walked over by the fireplace to talk to a couple of train employees who had helped her from the train into the building. The doctor was doing most of the talking and the other men were just nodding their heads.
>
> The spirit said that she knew that the doctor was talking about her. Because the doctor was a some feet away, she only caught a few things said. He said that she had a high fever and that he didn't know what was wrong with her. He told the men to keep her as comfortable as possible and that he would go back to his office and look at some medical books, but he would return shortly.

Linda said that the spirit told her that she'd died before the doctor came back. I am wondering if the spirit of this woman who died on the couch is the same black form that I saw come into the sitting room during our first investigation. I am also curious if this spirit is responsible for the activity that has been reported in the first-floor ladies' room?

INVESTIGATIVE NOTE

Just because something happens in an area that is known to be haunted doesn't mean that spirits are the cause of spirit activity experienced there. Case in point: during our second investigation, we had a team in the luggage building behind the main building.

Brenda was there, as well as a couple other team members. There is a big sliding door in the front of the luggage building and that is how you get in. It is the kind of strong door that has four wheels, two on the top and two on the bottom, and slides on a metal rail to open and close. This door is heavy and needs considerable force to either open or close it—so a gust of wind will not affect this door.

As you enter the luggage building, you are standing in a small room. To your left is another small room and straight ahead and on your left is a door that takes you down to the basement. The basement is divided up into two rooms. They mainly use these two rooms for storage.

Brenda and the team were just coming up from the basement, on their way out to the main building, when suddenly the door slammed shut. Brenda said that everyone jumped because when the door slammed shut, it made an extremely loud noise.

She radioed me on the two-way and said that the heavy door just slammed shut on its own and that I should get out to the luggage building as soon as I could.

When I got to the building, the team was standing outside near the door. After their nerves calmed down a little, one of the members opened the door and they heard laughing coming from between the two buildings. When they came out of the luggage building, they saw three of the train watchers and they were laughing their asses off. It seems that one of them decided it would be funny to slam the door on the "Ghost Busters"—I guess that was their name for us. (That's mild; we have been called worse!) The three of them were "three sheets to the wind" and I assume they thought they were being funny.

THE THIRD INVESTIGATION

Three years had passed since our last investigation at the Duran Union Station, but the inside of the building hadn't changed. They had done some minor repair work and some restoration, but all in all, it was the same as before.

The only thing that we got during this investigation was an EVP that Charles (another team member) recorded in the hallway just before getting to the room that had the ticket window.

It was a man's voice and you can here two people from our group talking. Then there is a pause and you can clearly hear a man's voice in a raspy voice saying:

"I don't know…no one said anything."

After again listening to Charles' EVP for a PowerPoint presentation I give to local libraries, I think that instead of saying, "I don't know...no one asks me."

A LADY ON A MISSION

Our friend puts on the Railroad City Comic Con and 2012 was the first year the event was held in the ballroom. We were scheduled to conduct investigations at the station over the course of several weeks to raise money to help in restoration of the Station. What better way to promote a fundraiser than to hand out flyers. So Brenda and I and the kids attended the Railroad City Comic Con and we had our table right as you entered the ballroom. We were the first ones people saw when they came into the ballroom. We had a clear view of the hallway from the ballroom to the attic door.

Later in the day, while people were attending a movie in the Board of Directors' room, near where we were sitting, I was keeping an eye on the hallway and the people coming and going. I watched as a petite woman, dressed in black pants and a white shirt, came out of the Board of Directors room. She was walking fast down the hall, hugging the wall towards the attic door at the opposite end of the hallway. I didn't see her face, but I could see that she had one of those haircuts that I think people called a "Bob."

My first thought was: why was this woman heading towards the attic door, because it was closed during this event? I was getting ready to get up and start walking in that direction to see where she was going when the woman simply vanished into thin air! She'd made it halfway to the attic door...and then she was just gone. I mean *literally,* she was there one minute and gone the next! I had a clear view of the hallway the whole time and never took my eyes off of her as she walked down it. After I saw her vanish, I thought back for a second and then realized that the people standing about in the hallway never even acknowledged that she was there. They didn't turn their heads to look at her or move when she came out of the Board of Directors room.

I sat back down and just thought for a moment, trying to remember everything I had just seen. I am used to seeing this type of thing, but it still caught me off guard.

Our friend Nicole works as a volunteer at the station and she happened to stop by the table to ask us how things were going. Brenda told Nicole that I'd just seen the spirit of a woman walking in the hallway. Nicole asked me to describe her. I told her everything about the sighting and described the woman.

Nicole started to get a little emotional. It seems that the woman I had seen was her friend who had worked at the Durand Union Station and had recently passed away. Nicole said that she would have been dressed like I'd seen her when she was working, and that part of her job was to bring things into the Board of Directors room when they were holding a meeting. Nicole added that her friend would always walk fast like she was on a mission.

The rest of the Railroad City Comic Con was uneventful and I didn't see any more spirits that day. The fundraiser for Durand Union Station was set to start in two weeks and I was hoping that we would have a good turnout. We were conducting investigations, three a night on Saturdays, for three weeks.

THE FIRST OCCURRENCE

During the fundraising investigation, the first odd thing that happened was to me in the basement of the luggage building. We were sitting in chairs and I was sitting next to the stairs that led up to the first floor. (I never did and never will like those stairs. I always see things out of the corner of my eyes on those stairs. I don't like them and refuse to sit anywhere else in the basement except at the foot of the stairs, so I can see what is coming down or going up.)

We had a small group with us—maybe eight people tops—and as I was sitting there, I started to feel like something was moving fast around me. Nicole was sitting a few feet from me and she was telling me that there were times that see couldn't see my face. She said that there was something black blocking it out.

Nicole then told me that she couldn't see my legs and it looked like something was swirling fast around them. I began to feel a swirling motion up around my chest; then a very cold air mass all around me. One of the people in the basement with me said that she couldn't see me from the waist up because it looked like something was surrounding me. I felt it and I had never felt this before.

This went on for fifteen minutes; then the feeling of being surrounded finally subsided and I started to get warm again. It was early in the morning—we are talking 3 a.m.—and you would *expect* a basement with no heat to get cold. However, this cold was just around *me* and, before I started to feel the movement around me, I noted that I was feeling the cold coming down the stairs. That was the only time this happened to anyone in the luggage building during our time there doing the fundraiser.

THE SECOND OCCURRENCE

The second occurrence was experienced by Brenda. She was bringing in some equipment from the outside for setup. Charles was with us that night and he always wears combat boots and, when he walks, they make a really loud sound—especially on the wooden floors of the Durand Union Station.

Brenda said that she was at the base of the stairs getting ready to go up when she heard heavy footsteps coming down. In order to go up to the second floor at the station, you need to climb up a handful of stairs to the landing, make a 180-degree turn to the right, then climb another handful of stairs until you reach the second floor. When you are at the base of the stairs, you cannot see who is coming down until they get past the landing. Brenda was carrying a couple of cases of equipment and it would be hard for her to maneuver around Charles on the stairs, so she decided to wait until he came down. But when the footsteps hit the landing, they stopped. She called out, "Charles, is that you?" There was no response.

Just about that time Charles came walking down the hallway towards Brenda. Brenda asked him, "Where are you coming from Charles?"

Charles replied, "I was in the ladies' restroom putting my tape recorder in the sitting area, why?"

"I heard someone coming down the stairs and I thought it was you because it sounded like someone had on boots."

"Wasn't me," Charles said.

We never found out who or what was coming down those stairs. It could have been any of the spirits that call the Durand Union Station home.

THE THIRD OCCURRENCE

The third thing that happened to us occurred outside the building. We had split up into two teams. My team was in the ticket window area sitting on the benches conducting an EVP session. Brenda's team was in the luggage building.

"Where are you guys?" Brenda asked over the two-way radio.

"We are all on the first floor near the ladies' restroom," I answered.

"So, no one is outside?"

"No," I replied. "Why?"

Brenda went on to say that when they were in the luggage building, someone in their group looked out the window and saw someone looking in the window of the station near the front of the building, near the train tracks, and they were wondering if that person was someone from our group. She said that the person was a woman, but couldn't tell if she was a paying customer or a train watcher.

I asked how long ago they saw this person and she advised that just a minute or so had passed. Immediately going outside, I could find no one around the building. I didn't even see any train watchers outside. I think that there was a spirit of a woman looking in the building's window and we just happened to see it. There just wasn't enough time for a living person to leave the area before I went outside to look.

We kept an eye on the front of the building during the rest of the investigation, in case the spirit came back. We did not see it again outside the rest of the night, but we did have something happen in the ballroom.

THE BALLROOM

Our daughter Jessica was at the Durand Union Station that night with us and she was in the ballroom watching the monitor for the video cameras. She would radio us if she saw anything that was odd from different spots in the building.

We had set up a motion detector in the room and it was facing away from the table where Jessica was sitting. She was playing music from her iPhone and

This is a still shot taken from video. You can see the shadow on the fence just to the bottom right of the light.

had the volume turned up loud—so anyone in the ballroom could hear the music. She was playing music from the 1968 *Spooky* by Classic IV to try to get any reaction from the spirits that might be in the building.

Sitting at the table by the monitor, she was looking at the artwork for the music on her iPhone and, out of the corner of her eye, she saw a shadow pass by. At the exact time she saw the shadow, the motion detector went off, and it was pointing in the direction of the black shadow. The motion detectors we use are infrared. This means that any kind of movement, even something that *we* can't see, will set it off. When the detector senses movement, it gives you a *ding-dong* type of sound. (If you have ever gone into a Pier I store, you know exactly the sound that I am talking about.)

She only saw the shadow for a few seconds and then it was gone. It freaked her out a lot and she made it clear that she would not be alone in the ballroom ever again. I think I failed to mention that all the lights in the ballroom were out, so it was pretty much pitch-black in there. The only light was from the monitor and that was just enough to cast a faint glow in the area near the table.

Our Best Occurrence

I saved our best experience at the Durand Union Station for last station. It happened outside the building, near the train tracks.

Before the first guests started to arrive, I was setting up the video cameras. We had one in the ballroom facing down the hallway towards the attic, another one in the basement of the luggage building, one downstairs in the ticket window area looking at the ladies' restroom, and, for the first time for us at the station, we put a video camera *outside*. I had it facing towards the luggage building.

When I am setting up video cameras, I always ask Brenda on the two-way radio to look at the monitor to see if the angle of the video camera is good. I had asked her whether the picture was clear on the monitor outside. She said the picture was fine, but asked why it was facing the luggage building. I told her that since we had the spirit outside last week, I thought that was where the camera should be facing.

She reminded me that the spirit wasn't seen near the luggage building, but instead, it was seen near the front of the station and asked if I could move the camera so it was facing the opposite direction. I turned the video camera around 180 degrees on the tripod so it was facing the front of the Station.

Again, I radioed after moving the camera to see if the picture was good. Brenda advised that it was and that we could see the train tracks, the ticket window, and the whole area to the left of where they had seen the spirit the night before.

When all the people for the last investigation fundraiser arrived, we went over the rules for the night's investigation, asked if there were any questions—there weren't—and then split up into two teams.

Brenda was sitting this investigation out, so she and Jessica were in the ballroom manning the monitor and taking calls over the two-way radios. Jenny, who has been a member for years, and I were the team leaders for this last investigation.

Jenny took her team and headed out to the luggage building, while my team stayed inside the main building and went into the Board of Directors room. After an hour, we switched with Jenny's team and they came back into the main building. The depot was dead quiet this night—yes, there was a pun intended—it seemed that all the spirits had gone elsewhere for the evening.

We switched again after an hour's time, but this time we went down into the ticket window area on the first floor. We had a couple of people from my team go into the gift shop and the rest of us stayed near the ladies' restroom and started an EVP session. We didn't get too far into our session when Jessica came over the two-way radio.

"Where is everyone?"

"My group is in the luggage building," Jenny replied.

"We have two people in the gift shop," I said. "The rest are near the ticket window."

"So no one is outside?" This time it was Brenda on the radio.

"No," I answered.

"No," Jenny added.

I was more than curious. "What did you see?"

Brenda came back on the radio, "We just saw a woman on video camera number two near the front of the building near the train tracks."

"Where was camera number two located?" I asked.

"That was the one outside that you had moved earlier. You had it originally pointing towards the luggage building."

"Okay. Where is the woman now?"

"She went through a fence," Brenda said.

I was kind of being a smart ass here, "Okay, so she opened the gate."

Brenda came back, "No, you don't understand. She walked *through* a fence, but there wasn't a gate. You had better get up here and take a look!"

"Okay. We are heading up now."

"We are coming up also," Jenny said.

A short time later, when everyone arrived, I cued the video to where Jessica and Brenda saw the woman and we all watched it.

On the monitor, you could clearly see the front of the building. At 12:35 a.m., you can see a black shadow moving along the train tracks. You see it for a few seconds and then it just disappears. I played the video back a few times, looking for any logical cause for the shadow, but could not find one. You couldn't tell that it was a woman, but it did look like there was a dress flowing as the shadow walked.

Jenny and Tammy went outside to see if it could have been a train watcher who had somehow gotten into the picture. We could clearly see them on the video camera, and you could tell quite clearly that they were people and not shadows. So there wasn't any doubt that a real person was *not the cause* for what we saw on the video.

Another possibility was that right after the shadow disappeared, a train did go past. We thought that maybe the light from the train engine was casting a shadow and that was the cause of the black shadow that we had seen. When I watched the video at home at 12:20 a.m., another train passes the Durand Union Station on the same tracks and it was the same type of engine. As the first train came past there was no black shadow near the tracks. So we could rule out that the black shadow we had captured on video being caused by a train going past.

A side note: A few weeks after the investigation Nicole told us that she'd found an old picture of the Durand Union Station showing the passenger loading area. The photo was taken in the exact area where we saw the black shadow walking! Was the black shadow we saw the spirit of the woman who had died in the ladies' restroom years ago? Was she still trying to make it to Detroit to meet her husband? We might never know for sure.

You can check out our video of the apparition at our website, though. Our web address is www.semghs.org. Click on "Investigations" at the top left drop-down window and then on Durand Depot 10-13-12.

A PRIVATE RESIDENCE

Author note: I wasn't going to include a house investigation in this book because I wanted to include places where people could visit and maybe experience something for themselves. But then I remembered that shortly after we conducted our second investigation in this house, the homeowners opened up the basement to people who were willing to pay money and were brave enough to spend the night in what was concluded was the most active place in the house. I cannot give out the address, because I am not sure the homeowners are still renting out the basement. If you are interested, however...Google it.

As houses go, this house was cool as hell! It used to be a funeral home, but it was empty for a number of years and, of course, vandals took things from the house. There is an interesting backstory to this house, though.

A few years prior, we were contacted by someone who wanted us to investigate her house. She was getting ready to close on it and wanted us to come out and check it over to see if there were any spirits there, because it had once been a funeral home. We set up a time and date, and she told us that if we wanted to stay the night and investigate we could.

A few days before the investigation, she e-mailed us an apology to let us know that the appraisal fell through and they were not going to buy the house after all. We were bummed because we were looking forward to the investigation.

Flash forward to this investigation. We always ask the people contacting us how they found us. There are many ghost hunting groups now and we are always curious as to why they chose us for their investigations. The homeowner said that the people who tried to buy the house before them had given them our contact information. It seems that the house investigation that fell through because of the appraisal a few years prior was *this* house! I always thought, because of this chain of events, that somehow we were destined to do this investigation in the old funeral home!

We entered the house from the side door and stood in a little front porch area. When you entered the actual house, you were standing in the dining room. There was a door located on the right side of the dining room that led to the basement. To your left was the kitchen and to your right was the living room. From my understanding, the living room was the viewing room when the house had been a funeral home.

The homeowner (we shall call her Jo) had a couple of friends over for the investigation. This is quite common since the homeowner is allowing perfect strangers into their home. I guess having friends over offers moral support.

One of Jo's friends had been at the home for a funeral and remembers seeing the casket sitting near the big window in the living room. Her friend also said that a couple of her relatives had their funerals there in the house. (Did I mention how cool this house was?)

The stairs that led to the second floor were off the living room. Upstairs were two bedrooms and the master bedroom. Right off the master bedroom was a small room that used to be the embalming room! (Have I mentioned this house was cool!?) When the house was empty for those few years, vandals took most of the things from the embalming room. When you enter that room, to your left is an elevator that would bring bodies up from the basement. There is an entrance to the basement at the back of the house and the people working there at that time would bring the bodies in through that location and into the elevator.

Jo contacted us because they had just moved into the house a few months prior and almost immediately things began happening. She has two kids—a boy and a girl, both under ten. They have heard things in the house and seen shadows. Their cat will follow something with its eyes that they can't see. But maybe the most disturbing thing they saw was when they first moved in. Jo said that they were still unpacking when she looked towards a wall near the dining room. On the wall were raised letters that formed the words: GET OUT.

I know what you are thinking—because, to be honest, I thought the same thing. They must have imagined this because it is too far out there to be true. But you know, we don't live in the house and we don't know what is going on there. You have to give people the benefit of the doubt until proven otherwise. Jo said that the words stayed on the wall for a few days. Then, one day, she looked and the words were gone.

Jo had a table in the living room set up for us and we put our monitor on it. She gave us a quick tour of the house. We then set up a video camera in the living room, one in the basement, another in the master bedroom, and the last one in the hallway outside of her daughter's room, looking *into* the room, since that was where the most recent activity had occurred.

As mentioned before, we use the free-roaming method where our members take whatever equipment they want (some even have their own equipment that they bring) and they go wherever they desire. We don't assign members to certain areas for a set amount of time. It is hard to tell people to stay in a small basement for an hour, when there is nothing going on there. With that being said, we had about half of our members head down to the basement; Dennis, Mary, and I went up to the embalming room (where else right?), and a couple of members stayed with Brenda to talk with Jo in the living room.

THE ROOMS

We no sooner walked into the embalming room when I felt a spirit there with us. I walked over to the elevator and felt another there. After taking a picture of the elevator, the image showed a bright orb floating about the car and near the cable. I took another picture a few seconds later and the orb was gone. Walking over to the center of the room, I sat down with Dennis and Mary sitting near me. We formed a small circle.

While we were sitting there on the floor, a very cold breeze could be felt coming from the master bedroom into the embalming area. Dennis could see a

Orb in an old elevator in the home.

black shadow behind us where the sink was located. He said that if you looked directly at it, the shadow would move, but if you looked at it from the corner of your eyes (in peripheral vision), you could see it.

Dennis took a few pictures with his digital camera, but nothing showed on them. Now, the cold breeze turned into a cold air mass that surrounded us on the floor.

I tried making contact with the spirit, but it wasn't ready to talk just yet. A few minutes had passed and the cold left the room and it started to warm up again. My knees were getting tired, so I got up from the floor and walked to the daughter's room to spend some time in there alone, since both of her kids were staying with friends.

I sat down near the door, just inside the room, with a clear view of the whole room. I was out of view of our video camera that was just outside in the hallway.

INVESTIGATIVE NOTE

A cold spot is caused by a spirit or spirits using the air for energy. They remove the warm air and all you feel is cold air. A cold spot may be stationary or it can move. However, be careful, because a cold spot or breeze may be caused by an open window, a fan, or the A/C coming on.

(There is nothing worse than sitting down after an investigation to watch video and finding that you have an hour of seeing someone's back because they were sitting down right in the view of the camera.) While in the room, I kept seeing shadows out of the corner of my eye. If you looked directly at them, you couldn't see them; you could only see them if you didn't look directly at them. We have experienced this before and it is quite common to see spirits this way.

I stayed in the room for half an hour, but didn't see anything else. My knees were getting sore again, so I walked downstairs to watch the monitor to see what was happening in the living room. Brenda said that they kept seeing orbs on the monitor near the couch and a few near the TV. I looked to see if the orbs could have been mistaken for car lights from outside, but none of the windows in the living room faced a corner where the lights would come into the living room.

While looking at some of the pictures on the digital camera that I had taken while upstairs, Brenda interrupted to tell me Tammie (a group member) was trying to reach me on the two-way radio. I took my radio out and noticed that it had been turned off. That was odd, I thought since I'd not turned it off. I called Tammie on the radio to ask her what was up.

She advised that she and Jenny (another group member) were in the basement with a few other people who Jo had invited for the investigation. Tammie had brought her iPad and she was using an app on it called "iOvilus."

INVESTIGATIVE NOTE

In theory, the iOvilus app uses the circuits and the chemicals in the circuit board and built-in radio antenna to allow a spirit to manipulate the app and speak through it. Our group is still open on whether or not these apps are really a good investigative tool or if they are simply for entertainment purposes.

For the Android phones there is an app called "Ghost Radar." We actually have used this app on investigations and we have found it to be useful.

For an example, during an investigation at a home we had investigated in Charlotte, Michigan a few years ago, we got the word "German" in the app. We asked the homeowner what that meant to her and she said that her ancestry was German. Then we got the work "Frank." The homeowner told us that her mom's ex-husband's name was Frank and he was deceased. Then we got the word "Zoo." The homeowner said that when they'd walked through the house when they were thinking about buying it, there was a chicken, rooster, and goat in the basement. They had joked then that the only thing they needed in the basement was a pig and they would have a zoo. The skeptics out there would say that this was a coincidence getting those words. But the words meant something to the homeowner, so I don't think it could have been a coincidence. What do you think?

According to Tammie, *somebody* wanted me in the basement. I asked her what she meant by that and it would seem that twice on the iOvilus my name was spoken. Tammie said that within ten minutes of her being there, "Brad" appeared on the iOvilus screen. Well, not one to disappoint a spirit, I got up off the couch and made my way to the basement.

When you open the basement door, there are stairs that lead down. At the bottom of the stairs, to your right, is a little hallway that takes you behind the main room in the basement—there is a workbench and some tools there. If you turn left and then left again, there is another small hallway that leads into the main room. In this hallway, there are a couple of chairs and a freezer.

Once in the basement, I found everyone sitting in a circle in the main room. Tammie opened the tab for the iOvilus so I could see the words that had been spoken and, sure enough, there was my name—twice. I thought that was cool, since I have never been called out before by any spirit.

"Okay," I said as I looked around the room, "You wanted me…here I am!"

I sat down behind the group on the floor and watched the room carefully. For some reason, the corner to our left was drawing my interest. After a few minutes, I kept seeing shadows dart towards us from that corner, then retreat back into the same corner. This continued for quite some time before I stopped seeing them. A few more words came to the iOvilus, but nothing that meant anything to us or Jo, who came down into the basement a few minutes after I did.

I was beginning to think that a crowding in the room could be the case here, since we had a small army in the basement. I stood up and made my way to the center of the room. The group sitting on the floor was to my left and I had all the intentions in the world of leaving the basement. The spirits had other ideas.

I had my back to the hallway that led to the stairs and, as soon as I turned around to leave, I had this overwhelming feeling that we were no longer alone. There were three spirits in the basement and they were surrounding me! I could feel them taunting me—and not in a good way. The spirits were like bullies that surround their victim and then walk around in circles yelling at them. I felt like their victim!

INVESTIGATIVE NOTE

Sometimes, if you have too many people in a room you can actually make it so crowded that spirits will not come in until most of the people have left. That is why we have found over the years that a room will become active when a large group has just left it. It is as if the spirits are stretching their legs, so to speak, and maybe they can move more freely.

I have dealt with spirits for a long time and I hadn't met one that I hadn't liked. But I didn't like these three at all. I immediately shut down my ability to talk to the spirits because I didn't yet know their intentions. I told the group what was happening and that I had to leave the basement for a few minutes—not because I was afraid, but because I felt overwhelmed by the spirits.

I made my way to the dining room. The spirits had not followed me and the fresh air did me a world of good. I just stood there for a few minutes gathering my senses.

I told Brenda what had happened and she said that I had better stay upstairs for a while. But I said no; I needed to go back down there to see what the spirits wanted since they called me out. After a few more minutes, I took a breath of air and went back down into the basement. No sooner had I set foot back in the main room when I had that unpleasant feeling of being bullied and surrounded again.

I stayed in the basement for a few minutes, but I couldn't take that overwhelming feeling, so I left, again. Upon leaving, I looked back at the people sitting on the floor and apologized for not staying with them longer.

The stairs in the basement are made of wood. You can easily hear your footsteps when ascending or descending. I was halfway up the stairs when I heard footsteps behind me. I made it to the door to the dining room and I could still hear the footsteps following me as I put my hand on the knob, ready to open the door to exit the basement. Then the footsteps stopped.

To be totally honest with you, I was expecting to see one of our members behind me on the stairs as I turned my head to look behind me to see who it was. I figured they'd had enough of the basement also and wanted some fresh air. But there was no one behind me! One of the spirits had followed me up the stairs to the dining room door. Maybe the spirit could not go any further. Maybe he/she/it was trapped in the basement for some reason and couldn't leave that area.

If an addition to a house is added on the spirit will not be able to go to the new part of the house since it was not there when he/she was alive. Maybe that was the reason the spirit didn't follow me into the dining room. Maybe that part of the house was added on after the spirit had passed.

I really didn't care what the reason was; I was just happy when I opened the door to the dining room and got the hell out of that basement. Brenda was still in the dining room and she asked me what was down there. I told her I didn't know for sure.

A PORTAL

We had never encountered this type of activity before and, honestly, I didn't know what our next step would be. Brenda suggested that I call Linda, our good friend in Florida who was a medium. It was possible that she would be able to give us a suggestion on how to proceed. When I called, it was lucky she was available to answer the call. I brought her up to speed on what was going on. Linda told me that she was going to put the phone down for a minute or two to see if she could "tune in" to the house and maybe get a feel for what was there.

Linda came back on the line and she said that she felt that when the house was empty, there were some people who had broken in and practiced some kind of Black Magic in the basement. She also felt like the entities or spirits there were the non-human kind, conjured up by the people who were practicing the Black Magic.

Linda said that we had to be careful because she was seeing a portal and there were many spirits coming and going from this portal. She advised that we would have to

INVESTIGATIVE NOTE

There are two kinds of spirits you may come across if you are ghost hunters. The first kind are human spirits. This type of spirit once walked the earth. This would be, for example, my deceased dad, grandparents, and uncles. The other type of spirits are non-human. They are the opposite of human spirits, since they have never walked the earth. These spirits are often referred to as being demons or the Devil.

Many orbs near a suspected portal in the home.

find the portal and try to close it. I told her that I thought I knew where it was located—in the corner of the basement where I had seen the black shadow peeking out. She told me that she wished she was at the house to help and I told her I wished that very same thing. Linda gave me a few other pieces of advice and we said our goodbyes.

With new advice now about the portal, I waited a few minutes before heading back down into the basement. Most of the people who were in the basement had gone. Tammie, Jenny, and Andy were the only ones left there. I sensed more than one spirit in the corner that housed the suspected portal and I snapped a quick picture. You can see in the photo presented here that there were many orbs in the picture. I think these orbs were spirits that were either coming or leaving through the portal. Either way, I had my work cut out for me.

INVESTIGATIVE NOTE

If you don't already know what a portal is, let me give you a quick explanation. A portal is basically just a door to the other side—the other side, as in the spirit world. Although you can't see this door unless you are a medium, believe me, it does exist! I have seen things come from the other side through such a door. The door opens both ways, so spirits can come or leave our world through this "opening."

Even though it is called a door, it might be *seen* as something else. I have also seen it as a literal hole in the floor; from it, spirits would actually climb out of the ground and into this world. I will tell you that if you see something coming from a hole in the ground, you don't easily forget that image.

I went over to the corner where the suspected portal was located and started the process of closing it. The first step was to figure out what kind of opening this was. I was able to determine that this portal was actually a hole in the floor of the basement with a diameter of about four feet. In my mind's eye, I could see the hole. (That means that, in my head, I could actually see the hole in the ground even though it was not visible to the naked eye. This is something you can only do if you are a medium as I am.)

The first step is to close the portal temporarily. This is the same principle as when workers cap an oil well. They cap it to prevent oil from coming out.

In this case, I am temporarily closing it to prevent spirits from coming out. Once satisfied that the closing holds, I will then close it permanently.

But here is where it can get tricky. If you close the portal, even just temporarily, and you didn't clear the room or house of the spirits, then they are trapped here without any means of leaving, if they'd entered through the portal that you just closed.

I walked through the whole basement and I didn't feel any spirits there. There weren't too many places where they could hide, so I figured they all have must gone through the portal back to their side. Since I had that one spirit follow me up to the dining room door, then stop, I felt comfortable that the spirits didn't try to hide from me in other parts of the house.

Since I felt no spirits in the basement, I had to work fast to close that portal before any other spirits could come over to our world. I sat down near that corner of the basement and started the process. I first said a little prayer—because I figured that couldn't hurt.

Just as I started saying the prayer, I saw a hand and then an arm starting to come out of the portal! I couldn't say for 100 percent, but I thought I saw a horn coming out also! I immediately said the Lord's Prayer and followed with our closing prayer. Whatever it was went back into the portal and I couldn't see it anymore.

I then started to close it. I imagined putting big concrete slabs over the opening. I usually use four to five on top of each other when closing a portal but, in this case, I used seven. I figured it was better to be safe than sorry. In my mind's eye I also used concrete to help hold the slabs together.

The slabs seemed to be holding, since I couldn't see anything trying to come out of the portal now. I was satisfied that it was closed and holding. I looked around the basement and couldn't see any spirits. Just to make sure, I walked through the whole house and couldn't see or sense any spirit activity.

We were ending the investigation, so we packed up the equipment and took it out to our vehicle. We came back inside the house to talk to Jo to tell her what to expect going forward. I told her that I was sure the portal was closed, but we would be back in a few weeks to check on it. If we found that the slabs held, at that time, I would close it permanently and she wouldn't have any more problems. We also told her that if she had any problems before that, to give us a call and we would come back ASAP.

We did not hear from Jo, so we assumed that things were all right at her house. She did e-mail us a week later asking when we were planning on coming back out to her house again. The date and time was set at the end of the month and I e-mailed Linda to keep her up-to-date on the happenings at the house.

A SECOND VISIT

We arrived at the house for our second investigation. Jo was anxious for us to make sure that the seal on the portal had held. We set up in the living room again and placed the video cameras in the same places as in the first investigation. Even though the purpose of this second investigation was to put a permanent seal on the portal, we always conduct an investigation in case something in the house has changed.

The first place I went to was the basement. I wanted to see if the slabs on the portal had held and also to see how it felt down there. When I first entered, I could tell that the whole area felt totally different from the first time we were there. For one thing, I didn't feel any spirits surrounding me and the basement didn't feel oppressive like it had on the prior visit.

I put our Trifield EMF meter on the floor and made sure that the video camera had it in the frame. If the Trifield goes off, then whatever caused it to go off would likely be recorded for us to see.

Orb near the Trifield that is on the floor, just before the Trifield started beeping.

I was getting ready to go through the rest of the house when I sensed that something was behind me. I turned around and took a picture with the digital camera. No sooner had I taken it when I heard the Trifield EMF meter go off. When that thing goes off, you cannot mistake the sound for anything else! It makes a high-pitched whine. I took another picture and looked at the LCD screen on the camera to see if I'd gotten anything. In the first picture, a split second before the Trifield went off, there was an orb just a few feet from it. In the second picture, the orb is gone.

INVESTIGATIVE NOTE

Just because there was a spirit in the basement doesn't mean the closure on the portal didn't hold. There is more than one way for a spirit to enter a house. One way is for them to cross back over from the other side. Human spirits usually cross over from heaven and non-human spirits usually come across from the other place, which is commonly referred to as Hell. This doorway is always open and the spirits can come and go as they please. However, non-human spirits are usually conjured up through rituals and they seldom come across the door from heaven; they usually arrive through portals and they come up from Hell.

Another way a spirit can come into a home is by hitching a ride with antiques you acquire. If a spirit is attached to an antique and you bring it into your house, guess what? The spirit is now in your home, too. Usually, the spirit will not cause any harm, but you will know that it is there. A house that had no activity will suddenly experience phenomena. It will be via subtle things, like lights turning on and off by themselves, hearing voices, and things like that.

This may freak out many people, but another way is by spirit(s) following you home, because it/they have attached themselves to you! This can and will happen. We have had spirits follow us home after a day trip somewhere or even after an investigation (see Maple Rapids Cemetery chapter).

We teach that spirits are *everywhere* and they can follow you home from *anywhere*. Notice I said "can"— they will not always follow you home. If a spirit likes your aura, this is one reason to follow you. It won't be because you are attractive, single, or have a bubbly personality. The spirits don't care about that kind of stuff anymore.

I walked through the rest of the house and didn't feel anything out of the ordinary.

Going into the old embalming room, I sat down near the elevator for a few minutes to see if I felt anything coming up from the basement, which I did not. The investigation lasted a little over three hours and we had nothing further happen—which is a good sign when you are attempting to close a portal. We packed up all of the equipment and kept out one handheld video camera and a digital camera. I like to video tape and take pictures when I clean a house or close a portal in case something totally weird happens.

INVESTIGATIVE NOTE

I like to joke that cleaning a house involves using Windex®, a scrub brush, and paper towels. Cleaning a house by paranormal methods simply means helping the spirits cross over and giving the homeowner peace of mind. We have been called to houses before where the owners want to move out because of the activity they are experiencing in their homes. First off, the spirits don't own the house anymore; the homeowners do. There are ways to help a spirit move on and you shouldn't have to move because of their presence.

There are different ways to clean a house. However, I should note that what you see on TV and in the movies—people running around the house screaming "In the name of Jesus Christ, I command you to leave" while holding a cross in their hands—is purely entertainment.

What has worked for us is this: first, we make contact with the spirit and find out why that spirit is still there. Then comes the hard part: we need to convince them that we can help them to cross over. This is more difficult than it might seem. We have had spirits that didn't want to cross over because they liked it where they were. Then we try to tell them that if they cross over, a loved one, a friend, or even one of their animals, will be there to meet them on the other side. This usually works. After that, we go from room to room, starting at the lowest level and working our way up, using incense to help clean the atmosphere—we use a sweeping motion at the front door to shoo the spirits out of the house. Finally, a little prayer is said after they have crossed over to the other side.

There are generally four reasons why a spirit hasn't crossed over. The first one is that they don't know they have passed. This happens usually after a sudden death. Secondly, they know they have passed, but don't know where to go. Third, they have unfinished business. And finally, they know they have passed, but they like it where they are. We have encountered all of these on our investigations.

I started in the basement where the portal was located. In my mind's eye, I still could see the concrete slabs I had put down and there didn't appear to be any marks showing that they had been moved. It seems that they had held. Now it was time to put a more permanent cover on the portal. This involved putting just a little more weight on the concrete slabs that were already in place.

In my mind's eye, I added ten more concrete slabs over the portal. Each slab I put down was a foot thick. I didn't stack them all on top of each other, though. If you do that, it doesn't take much for whatever is trying to come out of the portal to get them swaying and make the concrete slabs fall over— and the portal is open again.

Instead, I placed them around the concrete slabs already in place so that one end is resting on the slabs already there and the other end is on the ground. Then I just build up from there. Just to be sure, I piled on some big rocks and, for good measure, I put concrete over the whole pile. The more weight the better.

Dennis was there in the basement with me filming and taking pictures. I told him that I sensed a spirit in the corner farthest away from the portal. He took a couple of pictures and we looked at them on the LCD screen of the camera. There in the corner was a bright orb near a tripod that we had forgotten to pack.

I told Dennis that after we were through with the rest of the house, we would come back in the basement to use incense, bring out the Holy Water, and grab the stray tripod.

There is an orb near the tripod in the upper left-hand side of picture.

INVESTIGATION NOTE

Incense: It is like a mouse trap that sends out a sound that only mice can hear and this sound keeps them away. In the same principal, the incense we use changes the vibration of the atmosphere and the spirits cannot inhabit that area—they must leave. I would not recommend cleaning a home unless you know what you are doing. You can cause more damage, if you do it wrong.

We went through the rest of the house and used the incense, letting the smoke go into each corner of the room before we went to the next. After I was satisfied that there weren't any spirits in the house, Dennis and I went back down to the basement.

We used the incense and then the Holy Water on the portal and at each corner. (Just a sprinkle in each corner is all you need.) I double checked to make sure the portal was still closed and it seemed to be. We grabbed the leftover tripod and left the basement. Finally, we opened the front door and shooed the spirits out of the house.

I advised Jo that things should be better, but if things took a turn for the worse, she knew how to reach us. She thanked us for all that we had done. We grabbed the video, digital cameras, and tripod and left the house.

A NEW STORY

We had not been back and we had not heard anything from Jo, so I assumed everything was fine in the house. Then we "Liked" her on Facebook and found out something interesting.

It seems that she took the whole haunted house thing to a different level. Shortly after our second investigation, she started renting out her basement for the night to people willing to pay for the experience of staying the night in a haunted basement. She took it to the another extreme and bought a hearse to park in front of the house.

We found out that she'd had another group come out a few months after we were there, but from our sources, we were advised that the house was totally quiet! Our sources knew what we'd done in the house—the whole portal thing—and said that we did *too* good of a job closing it! There weren't any spirits left in the house. (We did our job I guess!)

I don't know if Jo is still renting out her basement or if she is still having ghost hunting groups come in to investigate. However, there is another story to this house that has never been told—until now.

We were actually going to be on the TV program *A Haunting* again with this house being featured. We were in touch with the network and they said that the house sounded interesting and they had approval to continue. We gave them Jo's contact number and they said they would call her, then get back to us.

We hadn't heard back from the network for a few weeks, but that is normal. When they *did* get back with us, they told us that the story was really good, but there was a problem. It seemed that Jo was very happy to have spirits in her house now and was even telling the network that she embraced them.

Wow, she'd had a complete change in her attitude from the first time she'd contacted us until after her investigations. When she'd first contacted us, she had been afraid for her family. Now she *embraced* having spirits in her home. (I should mention, too, that the whole television network thing was going on *before* we closed the portal. We actually contacted them after the first investigation at the house.)

So, the network shot down the story because their audiences wanted to be scared and this story didn't fit that profile any longer. But even though the TV part didn't work out, we did help the family and that is the important part of this story. Some people do this for the fame, some for the money. We do what we do to help people. Case closed!

THE OHIO STATE
REFORMATORY (OSR)

MANSFIELD, OHIO

While this location is not in Michigan, it is only a short drive away. We have been here numerous times and have met people and groups from the Detroit area, Battle Creek, and, during our visit in 2013, we met people from Grand Rapids. As the word spreads in the paranormal community about this place, OSR will be on almost everyone's "to do" list for investigations.

According to their website, the long history of the Ohio State Reformatory (OSR) began in 1861, when the field where it would be built was used as a training camp for Civil War soldiers. It was named Camp Mordecai Bartley to honor the Mansfield man who served as Ohio governor in the 1840s. In 1867, Mansfield was promoted as a candidate for the placement of the new Intermediate Penitentiary. The Intermediate was intended as just that: a halfway point between the Boys Industrial School in Lancaster and the State Penitentiary in Columbus. It would house mostly young, first-time offenders who might still be reformed.

Cleveland architect Levi T. Scofield designed the Ohio State Reformatory using a combination of three architectural styles: Victorian Gothic, Richardsonian Romanesque, and Queen Anne. This was done to encourage inmates back to a "rebirth" of their spiritual lives. The architecture itself inspired them to turn away from their sinful lifestyle and toward repentance.

The Reformatory doors were opened to its first 150 young offenders in September 1896. After housing over 155,000 men in its lifetime, the doors to the prison closed December 31, 1990.

The OSR is located in Mansfield, Ohio, at 100 Reformatory Road, which is just north of US-30. According to the 2010 Census, the Mansfield, Ohio, Metropolitan Statistical Area (MSA) has a population of 124,475 residents. The drive for us is a little over three hours.

The OSR has been the set for four movies; *Harry and Walter Go to New York, Tango and Cash, Air Force One,* and *The Shawshank Redemption,* perhaps the most well-known movie filmed here. The prison wall from *Air Force One*

From the movie The Shawshank Redemption, this is the halfway house where Brooks and Red both stay.

is still standing, as well as the display of paintings of the communist leaders that are in the central guard area.

The Shawshank Redemption was filmed almost entirely at the OSR. The cell blocks were built on a soundstage. In the movie they are facing each other, but the real cell blocks at OSR were built like a horseshoe, with all facing the outside walls. One of the volunteers at OSR once told me that there never was a wall safe in the warden's office and a hole had to be made in the wall for it to be in the film.

Spoiler alert: If you haven't seen *The Shawshank Redemption*, skip the following paragraph.

We all know the scene when Brooks was paroled and moved into the halfway house...and when Brooks says that he was always afraid and then commits suicide. Later in the movie, Red was also paroled and moved into the same half-way house. The half-way house was actually a room in the OSR and is just down the hallway from the chapel.

As with any prison, OSR accumulated its horror stories over the years. Two corrections officers lost their lives there: one in 1926, shot to death by a former inmate who was trying to spring his buddy, and the other in 1932, beaten to death with a three-foot iron rod in the Hole.

On November 6, 1950, the wife of the prison superintendent apparently knocked a loaded gun off a closet shelf and shot herself through the left lung. The next day she died in the Mansfield Hospital. It's possible that the superintendent shot her in order to spare himself the messy legal work and political stigma of a divorce. In February 1959, the superintendent himself died from a heart attack in his office.

An inmate hung himself in his cell in 1955. One burned himself to death in his cell with turpentine and paint thinner stolen from the prison furniture shop. Two convicts were once left in a cramped single-occupancy solitary confinement cell overnight; in the morning only one walked out. The other was stuffed under the bunk. In 1957, a riot put 120 men into the twenty solitary cells for thirty-day stints.

We have been to the prison a few times over the years. We first found out about it from our friend Dennis. His travels took him through Ohio and he'd grabbed one of those state travel magazines. Just so happens that the feature story was about OSR. We made our first trip there the next year.

HELEN

Over the years, we have captured our fair share of orbs and EVPs and I even saw my first apparition at the prison a few years back in the third floor admin section. You have to be careful with picture and videos, however, because there are open windows and bugs can get in. It is possible to confuse a bug for an orb. (Don't laugh; I have seen it happen before.) Also, you have to be careful with EVPs. The place echoes something awful and you can hear people talking from a floor below you.

One of our first paranormal experiences ever at OSR was in the warden's quarters. As mentioned, the warden's wife, Helen, was shot in a closet in their bedroom. The warden kept a loaded pistol in a box in the closet that he used for protection. One day, Helen went to the closet to take something from a shelf and accidently knocked over the box holding the pistol; it fell to the floor and the pistol discharged. She was mortally wounded. Some say it was by accident, but others say it was no accident. Her spirit is known to haunt the area near their bedroom. Charles captured an EVP in the warden's quarters during one of our first few times at OSR and we think it was her voice we recorded.

This was one of those years that we were able to bring in all of our equipment. Charles had packed up everything and was getting ready for the arduous task of trucking everything back down three flights of stairs to put it back into the vehicle. He still had his tape recorder running. Charles e-mailed me the clip a few days later and told me to have a listen.

Charles said, "Time for us to leave, Helen; thank you."

A female voice is heard asking, "Where are you going?"

They have flying critters in the OSR also. Bats have made homes in some of the offices. The place sat idle for a few years and they had some broken windows, allowing the bats to get in. They have replaced the windows, though, and there are not as many bats as there once were. (I absolutely hate bats— just ask anyone who has been to OSR with me! The problem with these creatures is that they won't leave you alone. You can be walking in a room and they will fly down and buzz you...and they will keep flying near you until you leave the area! There may have been babies in the area that they were protecting. But still, they are a problem! But like I said, there are only a few left in the place now. I would suspect in a few years the place will be bat free!)

Our most recent visit to OSR was in May 2013. We checked in at 7:15 p.m. and received our wristbands. People were still arriving and the pre-investigation talk wouldn't start until 8 p.m. If I remember correctly, I was once told that the OSR ghost hunts are considered a sellout at 125 people. That seems like a lot of people, but the OSR is so big that you hardly ever cross paths with more than a handful of people during the night.

The staff will let you take in equipment and flashlights, but backpacks are not allowed.

INVESTIGATIVE NOTE

It might be wise to eat before an investigation, so that you are not hungry. Get enough rest. Consider that many locations have peeling paint, dust, and other things you probably don't want to know about, so wear clothes that can become dirty without worry.

(It seems that people were taking things from the property and hiding them in their backpacks!)

During earlier investigations, a person on the staff (Frank—no longer there) would let us bring in all of our equipment, including the TV monitor, video cameras with the tripods, motion detectors, and anything else that we wanted. We had extension cords running all over from room to room. This has since changed.

Like I mentioned earlier, I saw my first apparition at OSR a few years ago. We were near the chair room on the third floor admin section. He was gliding down the hallway. If you notice, I said *gliding* and not walking. When he was going down the hallway, his legs and arms were not moving. I saw this apparition with my own eyes and not with a digital or video camera. Because of this, I don't have proof other than I know what I saw.

One other thing we have learned from all the years coming to OSR: bring as much equipment with you as you can comfortably carry. There is no worse feeling than being at the farthest point from the parking lot and your car and finding out that the batteries in your digital camera are totally dead, or you want to do an EVP session, only to find that your tape recorder is in your car.

After we checked in, we did the obligatory visit to the gift shop. They have many items related to OSR, like books and t-shirts. This particular year they had a new line of shirts tied in to *The Shawshank Redemption* movie.

There was still about fifteen minutes left before everything started, so we went outside to get some fresh air. Even though it was still hot outside, the breeze felt good. There are some fake cell doors on the grass near the parking lot and people were getting their pictures taken behind the doors.

INVESTIGATING NOTE

Our friend Charles has the solution to having all the equipment needed and I started following his example this year. He wears a tactical vest that has tons of pockets and, therefore, has almost everything he needs right on his person.

This is what I carried in my vest at OSR: a tape recorder, a MEL EMF meter, a digital camera, a handheld video camera, a twenty-four pack of AA batteries, a twenty-four pack of AAA batteries, and two flashlights. Yeah, it was heavy and all the weight made a red mark on my neck, but I had everything I needed for a successful ghost hunt.

HOT SPOTS

INVESTIGATIVE NOTE

If you want to know where the current hot spots are for activity, the best source of information are the staff and volunteers of whatever location you are investigating. They have knowledge about ghost hunts that have been conducted. In the case of the OSR, they may tell you that *this* happened over in the warden's quarters or *that* happened in the east cell block.

I found a staff member near the front steps and asked him where the current hot spots were. He said that they'd just opened the sub-basement near the east cell block for the first time ever this season. They were already getting reports of people being touched there and hearing voices when no one was around.

That would be our first stop for the night. It was 8 p.m. and a man from the staff came out to talk to the ghost hunt attendees gathered in the parking lot. He went over the rules for the hunt. One of the big rules was that they have a working prison directly behind OSR, so hunters can't take pictures or shine flashlights in the direction of this location—the people there did get uptight about that. Another rule was you couldn't take in a Ouija board or do any type of black magic while in OSR; if caught, the offender would be removed from the property with no refunds given. Also—I didn't think this would be a rule, but apparently you have to tell people this—you can't have relations with another person while on a ghost hunt in OSR!

After all the rules were explained to us—there was a whole list of them—he asked how many people had been to the OSR before. A handful of people, including the people from our group, raised their hands. Then he asked how many first-timers he had. The rest of the people raised their hands. I would guess that close to 100 people were first-timers that night.

He told the people who wanted to take the tour to step off to the side and that staff members would take small groups into the prison. The rest who didn't want to take the tour were free to go into OSR. Almost all of the people who were first-timers moved over to one side to take the tour. The rest walked to the front door and entered.

We fell into that second group. I have a tradition at OSR: every time I first enter the building through the front door, I put my hand on the stone wall and say "hello" to an old friend. I like to pick up on any vibrations that might be there. When entering the front door, you are just a hallway, a left, a right, and then another small hallway from the east cell block.

We were the first, and really the only ones for a good hour, in the sub-basement. The sub-basement is actually two parts. Down the stairs and to the left is the original solitary confinement area. We found out later, from some of the staff members in the break room that when a different warden took over, he didn't like where solitary was, so he moved it to its current location. If you go to the right after the stairs, you are in the area that housed what looked like electrical equipment and something that used tanks—maybe water or the boiler.

The original sections. An area on your left leads into a large room that is empty except for three chairs. The area on the right leads to a room that has a steel cage in the far left-hand corner. This was the room where we would experience most of the activity.

As soon we entered the room with the cage, we could feel that something was there. It is hard to describe the feeling, because most people have different ways of experiencing this. (For me, it was the feeling of goose pimples, but stronger.) Brenda heard a male voice behind her and, when she turned around, no one was there. She couldn't make out what the voice said.

One of the staff members I had talked to before we came down to the sub-basement told me that females seemed to be experiencing most of the activity—mainly being touched. It would stand to reason, because this was a prison that housed only males. Brenda walked over to the cage in the corner and took some pictures. When she was leaving that area, she said she felt something grab her arm, like it didn't want her to leave. It freaked her out a little, since she couldn't see anything holding her back.

There were four of us in the room with the cage. Patti and Brenda were in the main area, and Dennis and Eric were at the back of the room near the cage. Charles was near the window, which was just inside the door as you came into the room. I had the handheld video camera and was filming near the door.

As I was watching the video screen, I saw an orb move as if it was coming into the same room with us. Then it stopped, changed directions, and went out the same way it came in. It was as if the spirit saw us and said, "Oh crap," and then went the other way. The skeptics among us would say that I filmed a piece of dust. But this orb clearly showed intelligence by changing direction, and a piece of dust will not do this unless there is some type of air current—and there wasn't.

Dennis and Eric said that they also were touched on the arm near the cage. Dennis kept seeing a shadow when someone took a picture. When the flash on the camera went off, you could see a shadow right behind his right shoulder. After a short time, Dennis said he couldn't sense the spirit any longer and he

05.17.2013 20:36:14

I kept seeing a shadow near the furnace. I took this
picture of an orb when I asked the spirit's permission.

was sure that it had left the area. When you took a picture then, there wasn't anything behind him.

I went out into the main area and Patti and Brenda went into the area with the cage. Charles and Patti began EVP sessions. I took a picture and saw a shadow on the opposite wall near the furnace duct work. I took another picture to make sure it wasn't some type of reflection. The shadow was still there, but it had moved closer to me! I turned off the camera and just stood there looking at the far corner where I'd seen the shadow with the aid of the flash. I was standing right in the smack-dab center of the room. In the far corner, where the shadow had been, I could see movement. It looked like someone or something was moving towards me, thought better of it, and went back into the corner. This continued for ten solid minutes. I told whatever was there that I wasn't going to hurt it and I only wanted to take its photograph. I said that I would take a picture right in front of me near the furnace duct on the count of three. I then counted to three and took the picture.

The picture showed an orb right in front of the duct. I took another picture immediately after the first one, but this time there wasn't anything there. I thanked the spirit for allowing me to take its photograph and joined the others in the cage room.

Patti and Charles' EVP session was over, having lasted about fifteen minutes. Charles was listening to his tape recorder to see if he recorded anything. Patti left the room and went to the room directly beside the cage room. The time that we were in the sub-basement was perfect for EVP because there wasn't anyone else there but us. Brenda said that she heard the male voice again while I was in the main area. Dennis said that he was still seeing shadows near the cage and he was pretty sure that this was the same spirit that he saw in there before.

After checking his tape recorder, Charles said that he might have something. He uses both a digital recorder and one that uses tapes. As far as I know there hasn't been a study to determine which recorder will give you the best results. We have, however, gotten an EVP on one type of recorder, when a different type of recorder did not record anything, even though they were being used in the same room.

INVESTIGATIVE NOTE

The difference between the two types of recorders is that a digital recorder will store the audio file on internal memory. You can play the audio files on the tape recorder, but that can prove to be cumbersome. The easiest way to listen to the audio files on a digital recorder would be to use a USB cable and hook it up to a computer. This allows easy transfer of the files. Then use your favorite audio program to listen to those files. This will also free up space on your digital recorder if you move the files to a computer instead of just copying them. On the other hand, a traditional tape recorder uses tapes to record audio. These are the same type tapes that you would record music with in your youth and play them in your car or portable cassette player. Today, the tapes usually come in two sizes, depending on the size of your tape recorder—one being a full-sized tape and the other one a micro tape. Tapes are harder to transfer to a computer and usually require a special cable or capture card to transfer them.

Both types of recording devices have inherent problems. The digital recorder cannot record over the internal files, but the hum from the motor has been known to be recorded and contaminate the EVP session. The traditional tape recorder doesn't have motor hum, but you will need to use a new tape for each investigation. Even if you record over a tape that has been previously used, it is possible for some of the old recordings to stay on the tape, and this will also contaminate your EVP session. Additionally, you can record EVP with anything that records, such as a cell phone or a video camera. Whatever recorder you use is a personal choice.

Charles cued up his tape recorder and we gave it a listen. You could hear it as clear as a bell.

"Do you need our help?" Charles asked.

"No" was the response.

There was no denying that Charles had received an answer from beyond the grave. It was most definitely a man and it wasn't one of us. He played it for us again, just to make sure and we were confident that it wasn't any one of us.

We were still standing around Charles when Patti came back into the room and said that she had been recording with her digital recorder at the same time and wondered if she'd gotten anything. She took her tape recorder to the back corner of the room to listen.

A few minutes later she came back, asking us to listen to her recording. Sure enough, she'd gotten the same thing that Charles had gotten. There was Charles asking the question and the same man's voice saying "no." Now, this is not historical or earthshaking in general, but it *is* important because two different tape recorders, in the same room, during the same EVP session, one digital and one using tapes, both captured the same question and the same response. In all the years that we had been conducting investigations, we had never simultaneously recorded the same EVP during the same session before. This was one for the books.

Most of the time you can't hear the EVP until you play the device back later, usually after the investigation is over. That was the case with another EVP that we captured. I was at home watching the video from the handheld video camera I was using. We were in the cage room; Dennis was just to the left of the cage and I was standing right at the door to the cage.

Dennis asked, "What is your name?"

Then you hear a man's voice saying quite loudly, "Wow. Weird."

Those were the only two EVPs that we recorded that night at OSR. We'd had a flurry of activity in the sub-basement right as the OSR opened, but after thirty minutes or so, the activity stopped as quickly as it began. We didn't want to spend the whole time in the sub-basement, so it was then we decided that we would wander around the rest of OSR until it was time to eat. (They serve pizza and pop at 11 p.m. in the break room near the east cell block bullpen.)

We went to solitary confinement, west cell block, and the warden's quarters before eating. After our meal we decided, as a group, to go back down to the sub-basement to see if the activity had picked back up. When we arrived, there was a group of people just leaving the area. This could be a good thing, as I have mentioned earlier. In our experiences, when a large group of people leave an area, the activity sometimes increases. We don't know why this is, but some of our theories are that the spirits don't like large groups of people—too crowded in the room—or maybe the spirits were picking up a bad vibe from one of the people in the prior group.

We stayed in the sub-basement for a short while, but we didn't feel the spirits this time. Dennis took a bunch of pictures in the cage room area of the sub-basement. It was obvious that the place was dead, no pun intended. We then headed to the Jesus Room, which is located in the west cell block. The Jesus Room has a huge painting of Jesus on one of the walls, hence the name of the room. There is a room in the far upper right corner of the area that has a story to it.

If you are female and enter this room, you are supposed to feel like someone is touching your behind and inner thigh. We had a couple of female members a few years ago who swore they were touched while in that room.

The two female members who were with us this trip, Brenda and Patti, went into the "touch" room and reported that they didn't feel anything out of

We were getting an EMF spike. There is an orb near the floor by the door to the right of the exit sign.

the ordinary. The only thing that was kind of odd was that I couldn't take a photo of Jesus. Every time I tried to take His picture, the digital camera would shut off. I tried three times with the same result. Finally, I got tired of this and quit trying.

The warden's quarters were next on our agenda. We didn't carry the same equipment that we'd brought with us a few years earlier, but we did have equipment that would tell us if a spirit or two were around us. Brenda and Charles sat on chairs near the bedroom and I sat on one near one of the guest bedrooms, right across the hall from the warden's bedroom. The EMF meter started going off, so I snapped a picture with the digital camera. There, near the door to the other guest bedroom, was an orb. I took another picture and the orb had moved towards me. I took another picture and the orb was gone.

Dennis, Eric, and Patti had broken from the group and were walking around in the admin section. They caught back up to us in the warden's quarters. We were getting ready to leave the area anyway, so all of us decided to go to the break room. This was a good time to take a closer look at the pictures we had taken earlier.

Dennis was going through his camera looking at the photos he had taken and one of them caught his eye. It was shot in the sub-basement when we'd first gotten there, near the entrance of another room.

In the picture, there is clearly a figure, but mind you, we were the only people in the area at the time. The figure has on a dark shirt, what appears to be white pants, and has wavy brown hair. The figure has its hands clasped in front of him and is looking over his left shoulder. I am saying *him* because it looks like a man.

Patti suggested that the picture was of me. I was the only one in the group that wore anything resembling white pants. I was wearing digital camouflage pants. I didn't think the picture was of me, mainly because I don't have wavy, brown hair. But we all agreed to go back to the spot where the picture was taken and try to recreate the picture to see.

It took us a few minutes to find the exact spot, angle, and distance at which the picture in question was taken. We took two pictures: one of me looking straight at the camera and the other an exact recreation of the one in question with me looking over my left shoulder and hands clasped in front of me.

I can positively say without any hesitation that the figure in question was not me; in fact, it wasn't even close. In the recreation, you can clearly see that it is me in the picture. All of my details are clear and crisp, whereas the figure in the other one appears to be a bit blurry and a little out of focus.

There is a person in the picture who wasn't there when the picture was taken. Courtesy of Dennis Fowler.

Another side note on the picture: We went down to the break room and showed the picture to Scott, who is a member of the staff at OSR. He said that it was a good picture and that he couldn't explain what it was. So Dennis did indeed get an apparition at OSR!

We left the break room and stood in the bullpen, debating where we wanted to go next. Charles, Patti, and I wanted to go to solitary confinement. Since Dennis and Eric didn't want to go to solitary, we decided that we would free roam.

Solitary confinement is two tiers and is shaped like a horseshoe. We walked all along the bottom level without feeling much of anything, and then climbed the stairs to the second floor to do a complete walk-around. About halfway down, before ging around to the other side, we could feel something there. We could actually feel the electricity in the air, so much so that it made the hairs on our arms stand up.

We took some pictures, but didn't get anything. We continued around to the other side and ended up back near the stairs. There happened to be three chairs near the stairs, so we sat down and tried doing an EVP session. Unfortunately, because people came up the stairs, all we recorded were the footsteps and the voices when they talked. Sitting there for over half an hour, we just listened and watched for anything paranormal. Nothing really happened during the time we spent in solitary confinement.

There were two guys who came up the stairs and asked us if we had seen anything up there. We told them we saw a few things, but nothing major. They walked around the upper tier, but only made it to the third cell before they came back and stood by us. (I don't know why they decided to stay with us. In our many visits to the prison, we seem to attract people who want to follow along with us. I think it may be because of our equipment, that we know our way around the prison, and that we are a ghost hunting group.)

Eric and Dennis came up the stairs and met us on the second tier. They said that they were chased out of the sub-basement by something.

"Did something actually chase you out?" I asked.

"No," Dennis replied back. "We weren't physically chased, but you could feel the spirit, and he wasn't happy."

I was very curious at that point, "Then we need to go and see what is there."

We gathered up our equipment and stood up to leave. The two gentlemen who were there with us asked us if they could join us. We said sure and we all started walking towards the sub-basement.

We went down the stairs towards the sub-basement, but this time we went to the right at the bottom of the stairs. We came out into one big room with smaller rooms off the larger one. There were pieces of equipment everywhere and what looked to be one big furnace in the center of the bigger room.

Dennis said that the room in question was at the end of the larger one. As soon as we entered the room we could feel that something was there—and it definitely didn't want us there. We have never let that stop us before and we went further in. There was a door at the back of the room and it had a chain and lock that prevented anyone from going into yet another, smaller room. That was too bad, because you could feel more energy from that smaller room. As it was, the presence that was in there was really strong ten feet in *front* of the locked door. Dennis sat down on the floor a few feet from the locked door and I moved back about halfway towards the where we'd entered. Eric and the two guys we'd picked up were scattered throughout the room taking pictures or just watching what was going on.

Dennis said that he felt something was right behind him. I took a picture and there was a shadow just to the left of him. Then Dennis said it was gone, so I took another photo. This time there wasn't anything there. I put down the digital camera and started using the handheld video camera.

It didn't take long before I got something on video! I had only been recording for a minute tops when an orb came from behind the chained door, heading towards Dennis, stopped, and then turned around, heading back to disappear behind the chained door. My battery on the IR extender started to die and was flickering real fast—the battery was almost dead and it would be turning off in a second or two, which it did.

INVESTIGATIVE NOTE

The IR extender is an infra-red light that extends the distance that you can either take digital pictures or record video in total darkness up to 150 feet. By comparison, just the infra-red light on the handheld video camera alone is only good up to ten feet in total darkness. After the ten feet, you can't really see anything.

The feeling like something was there when we first entered the room was gone. I had to charge at least one of the IR extenders. I carried two of them, so we left the room and headed to the break room to plug in both IR extenders.

"X" MARKS THE SPOT

When both of the IR extenders were charged, we went out into the bullpen area to decide where to go next. On the bars that started the east cell block was an informational display that told the history of the east cell block and some of the more interesting stories about things that had happened there. One of the stories told how the inmates would play a game with the cell doors when the guards would close them. The inmates would stick their heads out of the cells and when the doors closed, they waited until the last second to pull their heads back inside the cell. The inmate who waited the longest won the game. The display said that one inmate lost the game, and his head. It was crushed when he waited a little too long and the cell door closed on it.

Another item on the display was the story about how the people from the TV show *Ghost Adventures* were at the OSR and they detected some activity in one of the cells by using a Magic Marker to put an "X" over the cell door to mark the active cell. The display said that it was on the fourth tier, fourth cell from the end. So, we started our trek to find that X.

There was a bit of confusion regarding which tier the X could be found. If counting the ground floor, then we would have to only go to the third tier, but by not counting the ground floor, then we would have to go up to the fourth tier. After some animated discussions, it was decided that we would not count the ground floor and would climb up to the fourth tier, going all the way down to the fourth cell from the end.

At this early hour—it was about 3 a.m.—our little group consisted of Dennis, Eric, Charles, Patti, and myself, as well as the two gentlemen that we'd picked up in solitary.

We climbed the stairs up to the fourth tier. One of the guys we picked up and I brought up the rear, while the rest of the group was a few feet ahead of us. We made our way down to the fourth cell from the end and could not find the X. If it was there, it would be hard to see through all the dust and other stuff found on the walls. We decided that they were counting the ground floor after all and that we needed to go down one floor to the third tier.

The rest of the group scurried past me and the new guy, making their way to the stairs to go down to the third tier. We took our time and looked into each cell as we followed them to the stairs. We were almost three quarters down the tier when I stopped and said, "Wait a minute."

We both stopped and I headed back two cells from where we were standing. The new guy followed me to the cell door.

"You saw him, too?" the new guy asked me.

"Yes, I did," I replied back.

The "him" that I saw was standing in the cell and he was facing the direction we were heading. Now, I didn't get a full-on look at him. I saw him out of my peripheral vision as we were walking down the tier. I couldn't tell you what he looked like or what he was wearing, but I know I saw him. The new guy confirmed there was something there.

I went into the cell where we saw the inmate and, while we couldn't see him, we could most definitely "feel" him. There was electricity that we could feel in the air. It could be comparable to static electricity and it made the hairs on our arms stand up. I asked the inmate if I could take his picture. I counted to three and took a couple of pictures. I didn't get anything on the digital and the electricity feeling wasn't there anymore.

We caught up with the group as they were making their way down to the third tier to see if we could find the elusive X. I told them what we saw, but no one else saw anything. This just backs up my claim that if a spirit wants you to see it, you will; if it doesn't, well, you won't. We made our way to the end of the tier and counted four cells from the end. There it was: the X above the cell door.

We took some pictures of the cell and a few of us poked our heads in. We didn't get anything in the pictures nor did we feel anything odd. But then this just proves that just because one group finds something, it doesn't guarantee that the next group will experience the same thing. Last year, when the staff was telling us the rules before that year's hunt, they said something that I feel is worth repeating. "You shouldn't expect things to happen as soon as you enter the building." The 'Ghost Hunters Academy' was at OSR and they filmed for over three days and only got twelve minutes of footage that could be deemed supernatural in nature. Be patient and you might see something odd, but don't expect it." I agree.

There was only an hour left in the ghost hunt and the only place we hadn't been to as yet was the library. We made the trek to that location and we were the only ones in the room. That made it easier to conduct an EVP session. We did a fifteen minute session, but didn't get anything. However, something strange *did* happen to us.

We had been up there for at least half an hour when the two new guys told us that they were heading out and they thanked us for allowing them to tag along. Then we started to take some pictures in the room.

The first ten or so pictures I took came out fine. Then I started getting weird pictures. I don't think it was a camera malfunction because I never had problems with it before or since. The problem I was having was this: every time I would take a picture, the flash would work, because I saw it flash and, in a dark room, it would usually light the room up, but the flash would only go a few feet and then stop. It was like there was some type of darkness that wouldn't let the flash go any further.

I told the others in the group of the problem I was having. They came over and sat beside me while I showed them the shots. Sure enough, it was as I'd said: the flash only went a few feet past the camera and that was it. I took more pictures with the same results. The others couldn't explain what was going on.

I finally got tired of all this and I said out loud, "I know that you are causing this to happen when I take a picture. I am not going to hurt you and I really don't care what you did to end up here in OSR. All I want to do is take pictures without any problems. Can you make this happen please?" The next picture and all pictures from that point on were fine and when the flash

I was having problems taking pictures in the library. I asked the spirit to let me take its photograph. There is a bright orb in the middle of the shot.

went off, the whole room was lit, like it should have been. The first picture, after I voiced my concerns with the spirits, displayed a nice, bright orb a few feet from me. Was this the spirit that was causing the camera to malfunction? We might never know, but was it a coincidence that after I asked to take pictures again that this orb was in the first picture?

We only had fifteen minutes before the ghost hunt was over for us. We gathered up our cameras and thanked the spirits for another good ghost hunt. The sun was starting to rise when we pulled out of the parking lot and headed to our hotel rooms for a few hours of sleep before starting for home.

Visitor Information

If you think you have what it takes to spend the night at a haunted prison here is some preliminary information.

The Ohio State Reformatory

100 Reformatory Road, Mansfield, OH 44905
(419) 522-2644
info@mrps.org
www.mrps.org./

OSR has daily tours of the prison, Halloween tours, and they offer the central guard area for receptions and, of course, ghost hunts. For the ghost hunt participants, check in at 7 p.m. and the ghost hunt starts at 8 p.m., lasting until 5 a.m. the next morning. If you have never been to the prison before, or just want to learn some history, the staff offers a tour that takes about an hour. If you don't want to take the tour, you are free to go into the prison and start your hunt. Usually about 9 p.m., they turn the lights off and the OSR is dark. At this point, you have access to the whole building, unless an area is taped off for safety reasons.

If you are interested in attending a ghost hunt at the OSR, just a word to the wise: they usually post the upcoming schedules for the following year in December. I would recommend buying your tickets as soon as you can, because they usually sell out all of their hunts.

A HAUNTING ON HAMILTON STREET

During 2009 and early- to mid-2010, we teamed up with Prozak, a rapper from Saginaw, and his team the Seekers, and did investigations at three different sites in Saginaw, Michigan. The sites were the Comedy Club, Perry's Schuch Hotel, and The Stable. The purpose of these investigations was to film us and to then put together a movie and a DVD with findings from these investigations.

Many hours of video was taken along with many hours of editing. Prozak and the Seekers did all of the editing and put the final touches on the DVD. [[How exciting!]] I should take this opportunity to name the Seekers: other than Prozak, the team includes Tim and Adam. All three of them were nice people and treated us very well.

The world premiere of the movie was held at the Temple Theater in Saginaw on two nights in 2010. The DVD came out early in 2011 and is still available online as of 2015.

The next three chapters will focus on those locations. I will also include a chapter about the Hoyt Library, which was used for an interview and promotion by a local radio station to help advertise for the premiere of the movie.

Without further ado, here are the locations that were used in the making of the DVD, *A Haunting on Hamilton Street*.

COMEDY CLUB

I won't get into all of the details of how the movie and DVD came to fruition, only to say that we were contacted in 2009 by Prozak to inquire about our interest in joining him on this project. The first investigation was to be at the old Comedy Club.

According to Prozak, the building that houses the Comedy Club used to be an old Moose Lodge. There are three floors to this building and over 33,000 square feet. The first floor has a dance floor, bar, commercial kitchen, and private rooms. The second floor has space that could be a dance floor and additional rooms. The third floor has an elegant stage, dance floor, commercial kitchen, and a private dining room.

The second floor space (that could be a dance floor) was actually a bowling alley with three lanes—the old kind where someone had to manually put up the pins after they had been knocked down. The odd thing about this area was that we found a spot that looked like something had been burned right into the middle of one of the bowling alleys about halfway down the lane. We found a small pile of burned material and it had scorched the floor a little. We couldn't see what had burned, but it looked like some sort of clothing. We never did figure out why, when, or who did the burning and what purpose it served.

We met Prozak at the building and set up our command center in the basement, opening our equipment cases and allowing any piece of equipment that measured the temperature to acclimate to the room temperature. We took some equipment for base readings and Prozak started the tour in the basement, taking us up the remaining three floors one by one.

This place was huge and the tour took over an hour to complete. We didn't get any odd readings with our equipment, but we did decide where to put the video cameras for the night's investigation. Back in the basement, three of us set up the video cameras: We put one camera in the basement, one went up to the third floor in the kitchen, and the last camera we put in the second-floor bowling alley. As usual, Prozak and the Seekers followed us with their cameras and we took some equipment and scattered all over the building.

Most of the recorded activity happened on the third floor—something occurred in all areas on that floor. A couple of things we could not explain and just to write about them does not serve the activity justice.

The owner and his wife were with us during the investigation. Unfortunately, during the whole event they were on the third floor tearing up the wood of the dance floor. They were using hammers and saws the whole night and this *did* interfere with evidence we were attempting to gather.

TOUCH AND GO

The first thing that happened was on the third-floor dance floor. We were to the far left, as you faced the stage, and towards the wall. Prozak was a good fifty feet from the three of us on the dance floor, as he was walking away from us and towards the stage. Tim and Adam were near Prozak, but walking in front of him. The *boom, boom, boom* from the owners tearing up the floor was starting to get inside our heads and we wished for the noise to stop. However, they *were* gracious enough to let us in for the investigation...

Prozak, when he said that something was tugging on his shirt

Suddenly, Prozak stopped dead in his tracks and told us that it felt like something was grabbing onto his shirt and pulling him back. We all went over to investigate and in fact it did look like something was pulling at his sleeve. You could see the fabric was actually being pulled backward, but there wasn't anyone or anything close to it. We took some pictures, but nothing showed up.

Standing around him, we could still see that his shirt sleeve was being pulled back. This happened for five or six minutes. The whole time there was constant tension on the shirt sleeve. Then, suddenly, it stopped and the shirt sleeve fell back down to its normal position.

We asked Prozak if he felt anything else strange and he said "no." He did say that when he first felt the tug, he looked back, because he thought that he somehow had become snagged on something. Then he realized that he was standing in the middle of the dance floor—and that's when he started to freak out a little, but he was okay. We waited a few more minutes to see if it would happen again; it did not.

Scott and Andy, members of our group, and I went into the adjacent dining room that was to the right of the dance floor and the rest of the group stayed within the stage area. There was a small room at the very back of the dining room that had hoses to hook up drinks and to dispense them. Right next to this room was a doorway that went into the kitchen.

A SHADOW

All three of us were at the back of the room when we all saw a black shadow person in the far corner near the door to the dance floor. We waited for someone to come into the room because it looked like a shadow being cast from the dance floor lights. We waited, but no one came into the room. The shadow didn't move, but stood just inside the dining room. I had Scott go around through the kitchen and see if anyone was messing with us.

A few minutes later Scott radioed. "Is the shadow still there?"

"Yes," I replied.

"I am standing on the dance floor just outside the dining room. There isn't anyone here."

"I can see two shadows. I assume one is yours."

"I will move; let me know if one of those shadows moves."

We could hear Scott moving on the dance floor and, sure enough, one of the shadows moved.

I radioed him, "Yes, one of the shadows moved, but the other one is still there."

"There is no one near the door," Scott answered. "I don't know what is causing that shadow."

"Walk into the dining room and let's see what happens to the shadow," I told Scott.

You could again hear Scott moving on the dance floor. There was his shadow coming into the dining room; then you could see him enter the room. We were watching the shadow the whole time and, as Scott entered, the shadow that was standing there simply vanished. It didn't leave the room. It was there one second and gone the next.

We tried to find an explanation for the unmoving shadow, but we could not. As we were standing in the dining room, we started hearing knocks on the walls behind us. There was one knock on one wall, then there would be two knocks on the far wall. We started taking photos but, again, we didn't capture anything on them. We thought maybe an animal was causing the knocks, but animals in walls usually cause a scratching sound, not a knocking one.

We even asked whatever it was to knock once for yes and twice for no. Then we started asking questions and waiting for an answer. Either the spirit wasn't in the mood to answer any questions or it was an animal in the wall, however unlikely, because we didn't get any responses.

TIME—IN REVERSE

Then, if things weren't crazy enough in this room, we looked up and noticed that there was a strange electric clock hanging on the wall. You could see the cord running down and it was plugged into a wall outlet. The odd thing about the clock was that it was running *backwards*. Everything was going counter clockwise: the second hand, the minute hand, even the hour hand. I can't say for certain that this was paranormal in nature, but I have never seen a clock run backwards before.

By this time, Prozak and the Seekers had wandered into the room. It must have been a little weird seeing three people standing there looking at a clock on the wall. Prozak looked at us and asked what was going on? Without saying a word, Andy pointed to the clock.

"What the f**k?" Prozak exclaimed.

"Odd isn't it?" Andy responded.

"What is causing it to do that?"

"Don't know."

This is the electric clock that was running backwards!

Now there were six people looking at the clock. We tossed some ideas around, but we really couldn't come up with a plausible answer. We all watched that clock for five minutes and it was going backwards the whole time. We could never rule out entirely that the clock was defective, but if that was the case, you would think that the owners would have replaced it.

SHUT UP!

After the excitement was over with the clock, I went toward the kitchen area and the rest went their separate ways. As soon as I walked into the kitchen, I was met with an ice-cold mass of air. I immediately checked for any source of the cold air, but I couldn't find one. I had a handheld thermometer with me, so I checked the temperature. The reading displayed 63 degrees with the temperature still falling. In the dining room, where the backwards clock was, it was much hotter than the kitchen, no pun intended. The dining room is right next to the kitchen and we were sweating in there.

The temperature dropped a few more degrees to 58. I started getting goose bumps on my arms. That's when I started to sense the spirit of a male that wanted to communicate with me. At first, the spirit wasn't in a talking mood, but after a few minutes, he seemed to loosen up and he started speaking. Once he started talking, he wouldn't shut up.

He told me that his name was Johnny. That seemed important to him because he spelled it out to me, J-O-H-N-N-Y. Now when I say that he was talking to me, he wasn't really talking to me like two people would carry on a conversation. It was like he put thoughts in my head, but these thoughts I hear in my own voice. I don't hear other voices—at least not yet—and I don't think that I am going crazy.

I got the distinct impression that he was talking trash and making himself to be bigger than he was in life. The Moose Lodge was reputed to be involved in the Mafia and Johnny was bragging that he was in that organization and that he was a ladies' man. He had claimed to have "chilled off" some people. I have to admit that I didn't know what in the hell that meant and had to Google it when I got home to find the meaning. "Chilled off" is an old Mafia term that means "to kill people."

But what stuck out in my mind the most was how he was dressed. He was wearing a full-blown, Mafia-style zoot suit. It was black with white pinstripes and looked to be custom fitted. He also had on black shoes, a white tie, and a red flower in his lapel. A fedora was cocked a little to his right and tilted a little forward. He was in his early 20s at best and I think he was still wet behind the ears.

As I mentioned, he claimed to be a ladies' man and he told me stories about his exploits. This kid just wouldn't shut up! Wherever I moved to on that floor, he followed and told me more stories. Finally, because I needed to have some peace and quiet, I asked him to please quit talking

INVESTIGATIVE NOTE

One thing I will say is to never second guess yourself when you pick up on things, no matter how insignificant you might think it is. It might mean something to someone else or may even help in an investigation. I also think that the more you go on ghost investigations, the more your ability will increase, and you might get to a point where you can even hear the spirits. Lastly, if you do start seeing or hearing things, or have feelings that you are being watched, believe me...you are not going crazy. This is just whatever ability you might have coming to the surface. Embrace it, don't fight it.

to me. I told him that he needed to move on and go into the light. I usually handle this a bit differently, but the kid was starting to annoy me. His presence began to fade, until he was gone. I don't like being disrespectful to spirits that take the time to talk to me, so I hope he is in a better place.

Immediately, the room temperature started to rise. I looked at my thermometer and it was reading 65 degrees. I checked it a few minutes later and the temperature was 72, which I assumed was room temperature. My talkative friend was gone.

BALLOON ANIMAL

When we reviewed the video from the camera that we'd placed in the kitchen, it had captured something odd. I will attempt to describe what that was, but I'm not sure I can do that adequately. It is much better when viewed.

It looked like the start of a bad balloon animal: it had what looked like three long tubes that appeared as though they were tied together. It was only maybe a couple of inches long. This thing, whatever it was, came out of the wall near the built-in coolers. It went a few feet into the kitchen, turned around, and went back into the same wall from where it came. I have never seen anything like this before and we have been doing this for a long time.

We finished up the first investigation at close to four in the morning, held our post interviews, and were all out of the Comedy Club at five sharp. The owners were still there and, when we left, Prozak thanked them for allowing us into the building.

SHUT OUT

Before the investigation even started, something funny—not funny then, but funny now that we look back on it—happened in the basement of the building. We had put all of the equipment in the basement while we took the tour of the building. There is a steel door with bars, much like a prison cell door, which is the way into and out of the basement. Somehow, when we were leaving for the tour the door shut. No one in the group claimed responseability for it, so I am inclined to think that the owners may have done it.

We didn't find out that the door had somehow been closed and *locked* until we came back from the tour to start setting everything up. There was a little bit of panic because we could see our equipment sitting neatly on the floor, and we had no way of getting to it. Prozak didn't have the key and he didn't think the owners did either. He was getting ready to ask them if they had a key to the door, when a couple of our members found a back way in and opened the door for us. It was a relief once the door was open and we were able to continue with the investigation.

Our night at the old Comedy Club was a great experience. The building was for sale when we were there, so I don't know if the same people still own the building. We would welcome the chance to do a return visit and investigate further. Next time, maybe there won't be as much banging!

THE STABLE

The building that houses The Stable, according to Prozak, has been many things over the years and was once was owned by C.L. Benjamin. It has been used as a livery, mortuary, and a fire station. It is now a store that sells outdoor equipment and clothing. The building has two floors and an attic that acts as an extra storage area. The attic turned out to be one of the most active areas during the investigation.

The first floor is wide-open retail space, with the stairs leading to the second floor on the far right. There is an archway that is a good twenty feet high and about twenty feet across, attached to the floor, which is made of bricks that separates the main floor from the rooms in the back. I am assuming that this was the original door area when the building was used as a livery. The stairway to the second floor is wide and has some elegant woodwork on the bannister and the posts at the top and bottom of the stairs. Behind the archway are the bathrooms, a break area for the employees, and a little storage room.

The second floor is divided into three separate main areas by walls. At the top of the stairs to your left is an area that had skis, bindings, and boots. Also, built into the wall is an area for displaying caskets when the place was used as a mortuary. From my understanding, customers would come into the building and pull out the caskets to decide which one they wanted. Andy took a picture where they displayed the caskets and, if you look in the center of the picture, he captured an orb.

To the right are two small offices. I assume this would be where the customers ordered and paid for the caskets. We went into the offices, but they were empty. (I was told, however, that the owners have a book that displays transactions for the caskets dating back into the 1800s.)

Continuing straight for a few feet, there is a storage area to your left that contains winter coats and lighter jackets and a room on your right that contains mountain bikes that are in some stage of being assembled. To the left in this room is a loft area that has bike chassis and rims hanging from the ceiling. There is a flight of stairs that go up into the loft area.

Back in the main area, and continuing straight, is the biggest room in the upstairs area. This part was added sometime in the early 1900s and there is still

The stable room is the room in the upper left part of the picture. There is also an orb near the ceiling.

advertising on one wall that was the original outside wall. This area is used to keep bikes that are still in their boxes.

To the right are stairs that go up into the attic and to the far left in this room is a small room called the "Stable Boy" room. This room is accessible by climbing a few stairs; the room is really small and was used for storage. When we were there, in the middle of summer, the room was unbearably hot. There have been reports of paranormal activity in the Stable Boy room for years.

The room was used back in the day by the person who ran the stable for the horses. Even though I didn't have anything happen to me while in this room, I will admit that there was an odd feeling to both that room and the stairs leading to it. I took a picture of the bike storage room. If you look closely at the picture, there is an orb near the ceiling.

The attic itself was a trip. The floor of the attic seemed slightly tilted and it made walking around a challenge. We always felt like we were going to fall over. Of course, we wouldn't because it was just an optical illusion. The attic

The space where they used to have caskets for people to buy.
They would slide out of the wall.

ran the whole length of the building and there were no walls there—only support beams—so we could literally look from one end of the attic to the other with no obstructions.

We did have some experiences in the attic, but I will go into further detail later in the chapter. Just based on the history of the building, we were hoping to have a good investigation. Let's just say that the building and spirits that reside in her wouldn't let us down.

The five members of our group—Andy, Autumn, Bryan, Brenda, and myself—all met out in front of the building on the night of the investigation and Prozak was already in the building waiting for us. We brought in our cases of equipment and set up our base at the bottom of the stairs and to the left, including our six-foot-long table with our TV monitors and other devices. Once all of the equipment was brought in, Prozak quickly locked the door behind us.

Unpacking the equipment that was temperature sensitive, we allowed it to acclimate to the room. Prozak introduced us to the owners and they gave us a tour of the first floor. We took our digital cameras and a handheld video camera.

They told us that most of the activity was on the second floor and that nothing really happens on the first floor. We concluded our tour of the first floor and they were right—we didn't sense any spirits on the first floor, nor did we get any positive photographs.

Before we headed to the second floor, we grabbed an EMF meter, tape recorder, and a digital thermometer.

We climbed the stairs to the second floor and it immediately felt different than on the first. The feeling wasn't bad or anything like that. Contrary to what some of the ghost hunting television shows want you to believe, not everything is evil or demonic. The sensation that we felt was that of being watched. If you've ever gotten that feeling, you know what I am referring to.

As we usually do at investigations, at least in indoor ones, we took base readings as we went on the tour. The first area was the room with the casket display. There weren't any abnormal readings there for EMF. All we were doing on the tour was trying to find the odd readings and to sense any spirits in the area that might warrant us placing a camera there.

INVESTIGATIVE NOTE

The digital thermometer has a laser that comes out the end when the trigger is pressed that will give the instant temperature of a location. This is helpful when you detect a cold spot or area. But you have to be careful when using it, because a window, A/C vent, or tiles on the floor will give you a lower-than-usual reading that might be confused for a paranormal cold spot.

VOICES

Standing in the area near the top of the stairs, we suddenly heard a voice in the small offices to our right. We couldn't hear what was being said, but it seemed to be a man's voice. Immediately after we heard the voice, we heard what sounded like something falling from the far office. Andy and I went in looking for the source of the sounds. Adam wasn't too far behind, filming.

There weren't a lot of things in the offices that could have caused the noise we heard. There were a few boxes on the floor, but with the amount of dust on them, they likely hadn't been moved in quite some time. Andy was standing right next to me and Adam was behind us filming when we again heard the same voice in the corner farthest from us. Judging by our reactions, I am sure we all heard it. We all looked in the same direction at the exact same time. Adam panned his camera over to the area and told us that he saw an orb move from the same corner and go into the wall that separated this office from the front office closest to the stairs.

Reacting to what Adam told us, the three of us went into the front office hoping to either see something or hear the same voice again. We stood totally quiet in the front office, but we didn't see or hear anything.

Joining the rest of the group back by the stairs, we told them that we hadn't seen anything in the back office. Adam did, however, tell them that he saw an orb on his video camera, describing how it went through the wall and into the front office. He described us giving chase, but not seeing anything in the front office, either. They, too, advised us that they had not seen anything come out of the front office.

We continued to the next area, where the winter jackets and boots were kept. Not feeling anything, we continued into the area where the bikes were assembled. The owner had advised us that the employees sometimes heard voices coming from the loft. Once, he said, a female worker said that she was working in the room alone, when she felt a hand on her shoulder. She thought a co-worker was trying to scare her and she spun around quickly, only to find no one was there. Now she will not work in that room alone.

We went back to the main room and on to the next area, which was the Stable Boy room. The owner told us that, in this room, the employees have reported things being moved overnight, hearing voices throughout the room, and having the feeling of being watched.

While the rest of the group walked around, Andy and I climbed the stairs to the Stable Boy room. As we got closer to the room, we could feel the energy of something being there. Climbing the stairs leading made that feeling more intense.

The room was small, cramped, and very hot. Just a few minutes up there and we had sweat rolling off us. There were a couple of printers there and a few other odds and ends. The distinct sensation of being watched and a very uneasy feeling was prevalent. We felt like we were not welcome and that, for our own good, we had better leave the room.

We still had the attic left on the tour, so we told whatever was there that we would be back later in the night; then we rejoined the group in the main room.

THE ATTIC

Some people in the group don't do attics, so they went downstairs while Adam, Prozak, Andy, and I headed up. We climbed the staircase and opened the door. Like I mentioned before, the attic is wide open and you can see from one end to the other. There are no walls, but the attic is sectioned off by support beams. As soon as we entered, we could feel that something was up there with us. I don't think it followed us into the attic, but rather it was already there waiting for us.

We started to walk towards the center of the room when we heard a loud knock coming from the other end of the attic. I was taking pictures behind the group and, judging by their reaction, I wasn't the only one to hear the knock.

Prozak looked at me, "Did you hear that?"

I continued to take pictures in the direction of the knock. "Yes, I did."

Adam asked, "Where did it come from?"

Andy was pointing towards the far end of the room, "It sounded like it came from over there."

I started walking in that direction. "Then that's where we need to go."

The three of us walked to where we thought the knocking was originating. The problem was that the attic, being so open, had an echo. So the knocks could have been coming from anywhere in the area. Once we were in the general location, we spread out to cover more area. I was near the outside wall, Adam was to my left and twenty or so feet out, Andy was behind me, also about twenty feet away, and Prozak was to my right, only a few feet away.

There was another knock, but this one was much louder than the first one. It appeared to be coming from the support beams to our left, which were about fifty feet from us. I immediately looked to that area and Adam was already looking in that direction.

I snapped a few pictures but didn't get anything. Adam was recording video and was looking at the LCD screen, but he also didn't see anything. There was a large crash ten feet directly ahead of us that sounded like something was either thrown or something big had fallen. The only thing that was directly in front of us were a couple of pipes and an old piece of equipment. (I don't have the foggiest idea what is was used for.)

"What the hell was that?" Prozak asked.

"I don't know," I said. "It sounded like something was either thrown or something fell."

Adam said that he thought something was thrown. "I was looking at the beams after the knock and I saw something in the LCD screen of my video camera. It looked like a piece of metal or something. It came from the left of the beams."

"Tell me you were recording," Prozak said to Adam.

"Yes I was."

We walked over to the piece of equipment and there was something on the floor that wasn't there just a few minutes before. A small piece of metal that was a few feet square and at least an inch thick was leaning up against the piece of equipment. We had a clear view from where we were standing before we heard the loud crash, and the piece of metal wasn't there.

You could see where the object had hit the floor and then bounced up and hit the piece of equipment because the dust on the floor had been disturbed. The metal object had to be thrown with a substantial amount of force for it to have made the loud noise that it did.

"I don't think it wants us up here!" Prozak said, half-joking and half-serious.

No sooner were the words out of his mouth than we heard another knock directly behind us on the outside wall. I had an idea and said, "Why don't we try to communicate with this spirit? We will ask it questions and ask it to knock once for yes and twice for no." This had worked for us in the past. Everyone was up for trying, so I started asking questions.

"If there is anyone here with us right now, please knock once for yes and twice for no."

Silence. Sometimes spirits are shy and don't want to communicate. It has to be a two-way street. If the spirit doesn't want to talk with us, the whole session is over. It is entirely possible that the spirit didn't hear us or maybe it was confused by our instructions for yes and no.

"Is there anyone here with us?" I asked again.

A loud knock was heard.

"Hi!" I said.

"Are you a male?"

Another loud knock was heard.

"Were you the one that threw that piece of metal?"

There was a pause, but then we heard a loud knock.

"Did you try to hit us?"

This time there were two knocks.

"Did you try to scare us?"

There was one knock.

"Do you want us to leave the attic?"

This time there was a very loud knock.

Adam spoke first, "Maybe we should leave. I don't feel like getting hit by anything."

"Okay, let's go," Prozak said.

I thanked the spirit for talking with us and that we would be leaving the attic now. I took a few more pictures as we left, but I didn't get anything positive on them. The four of us made our way across the attic to the stairs. I was the last one to leave and as I was about ready to start climbing down the stairs, I turned around to get one last look at the attic.

Right in the center of the floor space was a black shadow. (Just because the shadow is black doesn't mean that it is evil or the devil. It just means there wasn't enough energy for the spirit to manifest itself to show its real form.) This shadow was the height of a person and was just standing there, and I assume it was looking at me because, suddenly, it started racing towards me at a good rate of speed. I will admit that I didn't wait for it to reach me. I climbed down the stairs and closed the door behind me. We never made it back into the attic again during the investigation.

INVESTIGATIVE NOTE

There was an old four-story hotel in Louisiana and, if I remember correctly, it was in New Orleans. The hotel had fallen into disrepair and a new owner was found and that owner wanted to restore the hotel to its previous luster. No expense was spared. They replaced the fixtures, new carpet—the works. That's when the workers started seeing the spirit of a woman. It is not uncommon—in fact, it is normal—to have activity start in a location after remodeling has been started or recently finished. The reason for this is simple: If a location has a spirit in it, the spirit might be quiet until remodeling begins. The spirit may have liked the place the way it was. When you start changing things, said spirit might take exception and either cause trouble or show itself to possibly discourage the remodeling, so that the area can remain the way it was when the spirit was alive.

What is not common, though, is how the workers saw the woman spirit. She was seen walking the hallways numerous times and, each time, the workers only saw her from the knees up—the spirit had no feet! They found this really strange and the foreman began to research the hotel for clues about who this woman spirit might be. There were a few candidates because, in the first year alone, seven people had died in the hotel. That's when he found out something interesting.

It seems that a few years after the hotel had been built, they had problems with flooding. Every time there was a good, soaking rainstorm, the first floor of the hotel would flood. So the owners decided that, to stop the flooding, they would raise each floor in the hotel six inches.

When a spirit is in a location, he/she remembers the building the way that it was when they were alive. That is why you will hear stories of a spirit passing through a wall in a home. Most likely the wall wasn't there when the spirit was alive, so to the spirit the wall doesn't exist.

In the hotel, the spirit was walking on the *old* floor, which was six inches lower when she was alive. Even though the floor was raised, the spirit of the woman died before, so the new height of the floor didn't exist to her. She probably did have feet, but because of the new floor height, the workers could not see them. As far as I know, the woman spirit is still seen walking the halls of that remodeled hotel!

STABLE BOY ROOM

As soon as Andy and I entered the bigger room that housed the Stable Boy room, we could immediately feel the energy. Something was there, and considering the energy that we felt, it was pissed!

We made it about halfway to the stairs when we could feel a resistance. It wasn't something that physically stopped us, but we could feel the air had changed and it was heavier than when we entered the room. As we climbed the stairs, I started getting really hot and felt like what would be similar to the feeling of static electricity on my arms. That is how I sometimes feel the spirits. Andy asked me if I felt the heat and I told him I did. At least I wasn't the only one to feel it.

Once inside the Stable Boy room, the heat was unbearable. I could feel the sweat dripping off my face and when I looked over to Andy, he was sweating as badly as I was. We could only bear to stay in the room for a few minutes because it was so hot. Since we didn't experience anything in the room except for the intense heat, we quickly left the room, climbing back down the stairs into the bigger room.

Once down, the heat was gone and the cool air felt good on my face. The static electricity feeling was also gone. We felt drained when coming down from the Stable Boy room and Andy and I both sat down on the floor near the windows for a few minutes to regroup.

It was then that Tim approached us and he seemed excited. He wanted to show me something that he'd gotten on the video camera during the interview we'd done just a little while ago. He didn't know what it was he was seeing, but thought it was something paranormal and he wanted my opinion. Tim started playing his video camera, while we looked at the LCD screen.

In the video, you can see a spirit orb come from behind me, go over my left shoulder, and then disappear a few feet in front of me. It was an impressive video, if I say so myself! I told Tim that yes, what he had captured on the video camera was indeed a spirit orb and that it was a good one. Note: While this video didn't make it into the movie on the DVD, it did make it on the special feature section.

Andy and I started walking towards the stairs to go down to the first floor when Autumn stopped us right in front of the door that goes into the room where they assembled the bikes. She told us what had just happened to them while they were in that room.

Bryan was near the loft and Autumn was standing near the bikes in the middle of the room. They'd both heard a loud sound and then tried to find the source. A bike frame was suspended from a hook hanging from the ceiling and that bike frame was swinging back and forth. They'd walked over to the swinging bike frame, when they'd heard another loud noise coming from the stairs that led to the loft.

When they looked towards the stairs, they both saw a piece of a bike that Bryan said had not been there just a few minutes before, because he had been standing in that area prior to walking over to the bike frame—and that piece of bike was not on the floor!

They did an EVP session and stayed in the room for an hour more, but nothing else happened. (Autumn e-mailed me the files from the EVP session a few days later and there *was* something on the recording, but it was hard to hear what was being said. You can, however, tell it was a man's voice.)

We all spent a few more hours in the Stable, but the rest of our time was quiet compared to what we had experienced earlier in the investigation. It seemed that every place in the building had some type of activity.

The sun was starting to rise, so it was time to start packing up our equipment. I have always said that when we have an investigation, we *take over* the place, because we have so much equipment and use so many cameras. The Stable was no exception and we used over 500 feet of cable for the monitors and four wireless transmitters for the spots where we ran out of cable. It took us over a half an hour to pack up everything and that was with all hands helping.

We put the equipment into our vehicles and went back inside for end-of-investigation interviews with Prozak and, while he was filming us, we told him about our experiences.

We had a good time at the Stable and would like to return some day for a follow up investigation.

PERRY'S SCHUCH HOTEL

According to the website www.michigan.org/property/perry-s-schuch-hotel-restaurant-bar:

> For 138 years, the historic Schuch Hotel, located at 301 N. Hamilton has stood as an icon of Saginaw's Old Town district. Built at the height of the lumbering era and surviving various generations of ownership, the Schuch Hotel is a family restaurant and they have dancing on the week-ends.

There are three floors in the hotel: there is a basement, a first-floor restaurant, and the second and third floors are the old hotel rooms. The hotel is kinney corner from the Comedy Club!

The basement is your typical Michigan basement with a dirt floor. There are tunnels there that are unfortunately closed off now, but were rumored to have been used as part of the Underground Railroad in the 1800s. I know that Michigan was part of the Underground Railroad, but I can't confirm that it ran through Saginaw.

The second and third floors, which were once used for the hotel rooms, are now closed off to the public, but we had access to them during the investigation. We stayed mainly on the third floor, but did get to go into the basement. The third floor has some of the old fixtures and a lot of peeling paint. The owners are trying to fix it up, and one of the rooms on the third floor was available to rent for the night. The access to the second and third floors was by a side door and, if facing the building, the door was on the left side. It has its own key and, when the door is opened, there is a small entryway a few feet in. Continue straight ahead and there are stairs that lead to the second and third floors.

There is a main hallway that runs the length of both the second and third floors, from the front to the back of the hotel. Off this hallway are the rooms. I would estimate there were at least ten to fifteen rooms per floor, but the rooms were quite small—unlike newer hotel rooms today. There is a staircase that connects the second and third floors to the side entrance.

The Schuch Hotel didn't prove to be as active as the Stable was, but there were still a couple of events that we can't easily explain. The building certainly has the history and has seen the city grow from a small lumber town to the city that it is today.

We met Tim, from the Seekers, at the side entrance a little before 9 p.m. Propping the door open, we carried all our equipment up three flights of stairs to the room on the third floor that had been fixed up and made available for rent. In fact, that is what Prozak did: he rented the room out for the night, making it available to us in case we wanted to sleep a little before we drove back home. We appreciated the gesture, but declined his offer. It was actually a suite with a living room area that had a TV, couch, a couple of chairs, a bedroom, a kitchen, and a private bathroom.

We basically took over the living room and laid out our cases of equipment. As we usually do, we let the equipment acclimate to room temperature and grabbed some of it for the tour, so we could take base readings.

Starting the tour in the basement, the plan was to work our way back up to the third floor where all of our equipment was located. Tim went down to the side entrance to lock the door, so no one would wander up to the second or third floors, and then he joined us in the basement. The owner didn't want us to go into the restaurant on the first floor, so we took the back entrance to the basement. To quote one of my favorite movies, "Boys, listen. You're scaring the straights" (*Ghostbusters II*).

The basement was broken down into many rooms, but if you tall, you have to duck so you wouldn't hit your head on the pipes. I walked into so many spider webs I lost count. Still, the basement did not have a particular creepy feeling about it. There were a couple of spots that felt a little "off," but not anything too bad.

One of the employees did talk to us in the kitchen about some of things that he had experienced. He has seen shadows in the kitchen area. There is a side door in the kitchen that leads into the basement and once he saw a lady in a white dress "float"—that was his exact word—from the kitchen towards the side door and disappear through it.

We continued the tour back up to the second floor. Some of the rooms were missing parts of the floor and we really had to watch our steps. We didn't feel or get anything photo-wise on the second floor. Back on the third floor, we toured the remaining rooms there. It was just as quiet and we ended up back in the suite, devising a plan for where all of the equipment would be set up. We decided to put a video camera on the third-floor hallway near the suite and another one on the second floor landing where the stairs were located. This coverage would assure us that anything that moved on either of these floors would be caught on video.

But sometimes the spirits have other plans for us. We had set up the cameras, but hadn't as yet run the cables to the monitor, which means we couldn't record anything. This, of course, is the time that we all heard footsteps at the other end of the hall. Listening closely, they seemed to be heading towards the stairs. We scrambled as fast as we could to run the cable, but the footsteps ended before we could start recording! I still wonder what we would have recorded if the spirits had waited just a few minutes more to walk the hallway!

Not wanting to miss out on anything else, we hurriedly ran the other cable to the monitor, so now both cameras were recording—and hopefully the footsteps would return (which they never did).

We decided to head down to the basement to explore a little more thoroughly than we were able to during the tour of the building. Usually, we go through the tour pretty fast because it takes time from the actual investigation. Don't get me wrong, the tour is an important part of the investigation. But if we take too long touring, it takes valuable time away from gathering evidence and helping people understand what is happening in their home or business.

Some of our members don't do basements, so they stayed up on the third floor while Prozak, Adam, Andy, and I headed down. As we entered the basement, we turned to the left, took another left, and went into a small room that is behind and to the right of the stairs. As we entered the room, there was a workbench immediately to the left against the wall. There were tools, a few cans of different things, and some rags on this workbench. Against the far wall were various pieces of small machinery. There was a small area on the floor, a few feet from the workbench, that was mud—remember this is a Michigan basement.

On the other side of this room was another small room. We all went into this room and, as soon as we were all in, we heard a noise in the room that we'd just left. Prozak was the last one to enter and he turned around to look into the prior room.

"Did you all hear that?" he asked.

Adam walked up to Prozak, "Yes I did; can you see what it was?"

"No I can't."

Prozak walked back into the other room and we all followed. We were looking around to see if anything was out of place or had been moved. We didn't see anything, until we looked on the floor in front of the workbench. Lying on its side, in the mud, was a can of oil that had been on the workbench just a few minutes earlier. I know for a fact that it had been on the workbench—I distinctively remember seeing it sitting there because it was a brand that I hadn't heard of before.

The four of us formed a circle around the oil can on the ground. Being careful not move or disturb anything, I got down on one knee and looked at the can. It was lying on its side in the mud. It was not damaged or tarnished except, of course, for the mud that had splattered onto it.

Prozak was the first one to speak, "Was that oil can on the floor when we came in?"

Andy said, "I don't remember seeing it."

"It wasn't." I said.

"Then how did it get on the floor?" Adam asked.

"Well," Prozak said, "either one of us knocked it off or a spirit did."

Andy said, "If one of us knocked it off, we would have heard it and the person would have said something."

"True." Adam added.

I looked at the mud and I could see a spot where it looked like the can had hit the mud and then slid to a stop. The spot where it hit was a few feet from the workbench.

"Look here," I said, pointing to the spot in the mud. "It looks like the can hit here at this spot and then slid to a stop."

"Chalk one up to the spirits," Prozak said.

Everyone made their way back to the third floor now except Adam, Andy, and me. We wanted to look around the basement a little bit more. We walked over to one of the supposed tunnels and Adam began taping with his video camera. All that was left of the tunnel was a big hole in the wall that went in maybe fifteen feet and it was blocked off. I took a couple of pictures and Andy climbed into the hole, but didn't see or feel anything. Adam then left us to go back upstairs to change tapes in his video camera.

I took a few more pictures and, suddenly, the battery indicator on the LCD screen showed that the batteries were dead. That was funny because I had just put brand new batteries in before we'd come down to the basement. This is, however, a by-product of doing any kind of ghost hunting. The spirit uses your batteries for energy and, usually, if you leave the area for a few minutes, your device will show fresh batteries again.

At this point, Adam came back down and started filming us again, now discussing the battery issues with us. I took a few more pictures and, again, my camera displayed that I was low on battery power. All this was captured on film.

SLAVES

I felt that there was at least one spirit, possibly three, that were hiding in the tunnel area. One was African American and dressed in rags. He would peek his head around the corner and look at us, then slip back into the shadows. This happened for a few minutes. When I could see him again—and when I say see him, he wasn't physically there, but I could see him in my mind's eye—I told Andy to snap a picture, because I could see him looking at us. Andy immediately took a picture and looked at his LCD screen on his camera. In the picture, right where I told him the spirit was, there were two orbs.

Adam was still filming, including Andy and the picture that he had taken. Then I told Adam that the spirit was talking to me.

I said, "Freedom. The spirit wants freedom!"

We stayed there for a little while longer, but I didn't see or sense the spirit was there any longer.

A week or so after the investigation, Prozak called to tell me that Adam had captured something on video in the basement that happened when I was talking

Here is the tunnel where I saw the spirits of the slaves heading to freedom. We also captured an EVP that said "Freedom." Courtesy of Andrew Szalony.

to the spirit in the tunnel. On video, you can hear me say that there was a spirit in the tunnel and that it was talking to me. Prozak said that he could hear Adam ask me what the spirit was saying and me clearly responding: "Freedom...." There was a pause and the camera picked up a voice whispering "Freedom"!

No one said "freedom" other than me, and I didn't say it in a whisper.

Adam had captured an EVP of a spirit that I assume was a slave trying to escape to freedom. This just shows that you can capture EVP on any piece of equipment that can record. I was just happy that we were able to get this on video. (The video clip of the EVP is on our DVD.)

INVESTIGATIVE NOTE

The first rule when you are conducting an EVP session is never to whisper; always speak in a normal voice. A whisper can be mistaken for an EVP.

When we'd finished in the basement, we returned to the third floor. There was only an hour or so before the sun came up, so the decision was made to pack it up and head home. It took us forty-five minutes to pack up everything and take it out to our vehicles. Let me tell you that climbing up and down those stairs taking the equipment out after spending nine hours doing the investigation sucked!

Prozak had set up a room next to the suite for the exit interviews and, as usual, he taped the whole thing for possible use in the movie. The interviews lasted for a half hour or so and then we all left, except for the Seekers who stayed after to do more filming. Prozak was in touch with me after this investigation and told me some of the things that they had captured in visits they made to the hotel in the days after. (See the movie for more details.)

This was the last investigation we did for the movie and DVD.

Visitor Information

PERRY'S SCHUCH HOTEL (RESTAURANT)
301 North Hamilton Street, Saginaw, MI 48602
988-799-2539

HOYT LIBRARY

Note: This would qualify as a mini-investigation, but it wasn't included on the DVD. Prozak was doing a promotion with two local radio stations in Saginaw—Z93, The Rock Station, and WIOG 102.5—to help get the word out about the movie.

The Hoyt Library has a history of having paranormal activity and there have been numerous ghost hunting groups there conducting investigations over the years. The library looks like a castle, so that adds to the feeling of the place.

When I arrived for our investigation, it seemed that all of the doors were locked. Finally finding the one that was open, I went in. There were people standing around in one room—either there was something going on that I wasn't aware of, or I was in the wrong place. It turned out that I was in the right place, though. Unbeknownst to me, the radio station had run a contest where the lucky winners would be at the library on the night of the investigation/promotional event. (It would have been nice if we were told about this beforehand, but it worked out well in the end.)

Brenda, Autumn, and our two kids were able to carry all of the equipment into the library with one trip, setting up in a cozy room that had a fireplace in the center. We didn't want to set up too many cameras, since there were many people walking in the library and we didn't want people tripping over the cables.

Just outside our setup room, past a set of double doors, were stairs that led to the second floor. There had been reports of strange things in this area, so we set up a camera in this location facing the stairs and another one just past the fireplace looking towards the double doors. This way, if anything were to enter or leave the room through the double doors we would have it on video. These were the only two cameras we used. However, we did take with us an EMF meter, a tape recorder, and a handheld video camera when we went through the different areas of the library.

We only experienced two things while in the library and, coincidentally, both events happened in the same area, less than fifty feet apart.

THING ONE & THING TWO

The first thing that happened to us was in one of the reading rooms on the second floor. This room was just past the stairs where we had one of the cameras positioned. Adam, one of the Seekers, was filming me, and my son Sam had a digital camera. We were walking around the reading room when I sensed that there was a spirit right behind Adam. I told Adam that he had a spirit behind him and he moved to try and get the spirit on video.

Ethel

I said that the spirit was now near me and that she said her name was "Ethel." She told me that she used to work at the library at one time as a librarian and used to love it there. The whole time I was talking to Ethel, Adam was filming me.

I was talking to Ethel in the reading room. She is the bright orb to the right of me. Adam is filming with a video camera. Courtesy of Sam Mikulka.

Sam started taking pictures with the digital and it took him a few shots before he got something. In the photo you can see Adam filming me—I'm on the left side of the picture. In between Adam and me is a bright, oblong-shaped light. This, I believe, is Ethel, and a good example of a spirit orb. It isn't a bug and it couldn't be a reflection from the flash of the camera, since the light seems to be floating in the air between us. The shape is oblong because the spirit orb was moving and I think it was moving towards me when the picture was taken. I finished talking to Ethel and I sensed that she moved to another location in the library. I didn't sense her spirit for the rest of the night.

A few minutes after Ethel moved to a different location in the library, we scattered and Sam and I went down to the basement area. There on the wall were photographs of past employees and in one of the photos there was a woman by the name of Ethel. She looked exactly like the woman that I was talking to in my mind's eye! If I remember correctly, she died in the 1950s and was the head librarian at one point while she worked here.

THE OFFICE SPIRIT

In the reading room, where we first met Ethel, there is a door that leads to the stairs that takes you down to the first floor. If you don't go down the stairs, but go a few feet straight ahead instead, there is a door that opens into a small office. The office has only one way in or out, and that is through this door.

GHOST HUNTING IN MICHIGAN

We were taking a break from the investigation and Adam, Tim, Sam, and I were sitting on the floor in the reading room talking. I had a clear view of the stairs and the door to the small office across the way. As we were talking, I looked out of the room toward the top of the stairs and saw a man walk into the office. He had a medium build, brown hair, and was wearing blue jeans and a navy-blue suit jacket. I only saw him from the back, so I can't tell you what he looked like.

I didn't think anything of this because one of the DJ's from the radio station was dressed in a similar way and I thought this was him exploring the library. A few minutes went by and the real DJ came walking by us with a few people following him. They all went into the office. I watched the door to the office the whole time they were in there.

After a few minutes, the DJ and his entourage came out. I waited for the first guy, who I had seen go into the office, to come out—the one dressed like the DJ. I watched the door for a few more minutes. It had been at least five minutes and no one else had come out. The office wasn't that big and there wasn't much that one could do in there for this amount of time.

I walked briskly—not running mind you—to the office with Sam, Adam, and Tim right behind me. I poked my head into the office and there wasn't anyone inside. The one way in or out of the office I was blocking at the moment. I stepped back out and Sam, Adam, and Tim were waiting there for me.

"What's going on?" Tim asked with a quizzical look on his face.

"Where did he go?" I asked the three of them.

"Where did who go?" Sam asked.

"Didn't you see him?" I asked. "He went into this office before the DJ did, but didn't come out."

"I didn't see anyone," Adam chimed in.

"Me either," Sam said.

"Ditto," Tim added.

I looked at all three of them and, by their expression, they must have thought I was losing it. So I explained to them what I had seen. After I was finished, all three of them kind of just nodded their heads at me. We left the area and headed down to the basement for one last look around.

We spent a half hour or so in the basement, but nothing happened to us, nor did we see anything. It was getting late and the DJs were ready to call it a night. I wanted to go to the reading room one more time to see if Ethel was there. She wasn't, so we headed back to the room that had our equipment to pack things up.

With all of the equipment packed finally, we started the walk back across the street to our vehicle. After we put the equipment away, we went back to the library to catch up with Prozak in the basement. He told us that he would meet us in a few days to go over everything that we had collected from the three investigations.

Note: Prozak showed the movie we'd taken part in over two nights in October 2010 at the Temple Theater in Saginaw, Michigan. Both nights the theater was packed and it was fun to sit in the audience and watch everyone's reaction to certain parts of the movie.

Both nights we arrived early to the showing and basically had free roam of the place. We went all over the theater, from the very top seats in the balcony to backstage. There were a few spots where we had the feeling that someone was watching us, but there wasn't anyone around. This might be a place for a future investigation.

CONCLUSION

Everything that you have just read really happened. Nothing was added for effect or dramatization. While not all investigations that we have conducted over the years have provided results like the ones you have just read about, they are no more or less important than the investigations that didn't make this book.

We have been conducting investigations for nineteen years as of the summer of 2015. We have no plans to stop anytime soon.

ACKNOWLEDGMENTS

We would like to thank all of the people we have met over the years for their stories and experiences, as well as to all of the people who have let us into their homes to conduct investigations.

To our members: we could not have done this for as long as we have without all of you!

We thank the owners and staff of: The Purple Rose Theater, Durand Union Station, The Ohio State Reformatory, Comedy Club, The Stable, the Perry's Schuck Hotel, and the Hoyt Library.

We extend our appreciation to Prozak and the Seekers (Adam and Tim). Thanks for having us along for the ride...it was fun.

Finally, we would like to thank you, the reader, for going on this journey with us. Here is to another nineteen years!